Governing
Narratives

Governing Narratives

Symbolic Politics and Policy Change

Hugh T. Miller

THE UNIVERSITY OF ALABAMA PRESS
Tuscaloosa

Copyright © 2012
The University of Alabama Press
Tuscaloosa, Alabama 35487-0380
All rights reserved
Manufactured in the United States of America

Typeface: Garamond

Cover design: Erin Bradley Dangar/Dangar Design

∞
The paper on which this book is printed meets the minimum requirements
of American National Standard for Information Sciences—Permanence of
Paper for Printed Library Materials, ANSI Z39.48-1984.

Library of Congress Cataloging-in-Publication Data

Miller, Hugh T. (Hugh Theodore), 1953-
Governing narratives : symbolic politics and policy change / Hugh T. Miller.
p. cm. — (Public administration: criticism & creativity)
Includes bibliographical references and index.
ISBN 978-0-8173-1773-7 (trade cloth : alk. paper) — ISBN 978-0-8173-8628-3
(ebook)
1. Public administration. 2. Policy sciences. 3. Political planning.
4. Communication in politics. I. Title.
JF1525.P6M67 2012
320.6—dc23
2012011882

Contents

Acknowledgments

This project began as an article manuscript that *Critical Policy Studies* editor Stephen Griggs urged me to revise and resubmit in response to anonymous reviewer comments. I gave it a try. Problem was, by the time I responded to the issues raised in the reviews, the manuscript had expanded to 50 pages, too many for a typical journal article. Nonetheless, I am grateful to the anonymous reviewers of that manuscript for their comments and suggestions that helped get this book on its way. I applied for a leave of absence from my teaching and administrative duties to focus on scholarly research for a year in 2007–2008, which was granted by Rosalyn Y. Carter, dean of the College of Design and Social Inquiry at Florida Atlantic University. I am grateful to Dean Carter for that needed break in administrative responsibilities (I was director of the School of Public Administration at the time) and especially grateful for her support in the eventual acceptance of my research proposal for this book. I thank my colleague Ron Nyhan, who graciously served as director of the school during my research leave of absence.

Elements of this book were presented as conference papers at the Interpretive Policy Analysis conference in Amsterdam in 2007, Essex in 2008, and in Grenoble in 2010. Other parts were presented at the Public Administration Theory Network's conferences in Richmond in 2010 and in Norfolk in 2011. In connection with the 2007 Amsterdam conference, Henk Wagenaar hosted a workshop at the University of Leiden where several of us sat around a large conference table all day and discussed Jason Glynos and David Howarth's (2007) *Logics of Critical Explanation* as well as a draft of Wagenaar's (2011) *Meaning in Action.* That workshop and those conferences were sources of encouragement for me.

I want especially to thank readers of early versions of this manuscript for taking on what was still a badly organized treatise and for making helpful suggestions. Efraim Ben-Zadok at Florida Atlantic University, Gregg Cawley at University of Wyoming, Joseph Damrell at Northland College, and Mike Spicer at Cleveland State University read early drafts and, despite this, gave me inspiration and reassurance. Professor Spicer's careful reading and attentive critiques of various iterations of the manuscript were extraordinarily astute and helpful. The book is more coherent and understandable because of his critical nudges that improved the focus and organization of the manuscript. Tom Catlaw of Arizona State University also has my special appreciation for his insightful and thorough reading of the draft manuscript. I am grateful to Peggy Somers of the University of Michigan for her help with some of the finishing touches. And I appreciate the encouragement and intuitive genius of Camilla Stivers, editor of the series; thank you, too, Cam, for organizing this series in the first place.

Never have I seen such attentive and insightful reviews as those written by the anonymous reviewers of The University of Alabama Press. I am usually not an absolutist, but in this case I am absolutely certain that the final version is better because of these very helpful critiques. Dan Waterman of The University of Alabama Press was integral to the initiation of this series, and I am appreciative for his expertise in guiding this manuscript through the review and publication process. Susan G. Harris's superlative copyediting and careful reading of the manuscript are much appreciated.

I am grateful to the Florida Atlantic University doctoral students who commented on the manuscript before I sent it to The University of Alabama Press. These reviewers included Schnequa (Nikki) Diggs, Stacey Masden, Mariana O'Brien, Jean Pierre, Alexandru Roman, and Denise Vienne. I thank my sister Marga Perkins, who provided supportive critiques of portions of the manuscript. I would also like to thank the doctoral students in Gary Marshall's seminars at University of Nebraska for our joint Internet colloquia on some of the questions addressed in this book, on symbolization in December 2008 and structuration theory in March 2011. Similarly, I appreciate the energizing discussions with Old Dominion University doctoral students in Mohamad Alkadry's seminar in April 2011.

Finally, I am grateful to you, the reader, for the effort you will put forth to entertain the ideas advanced in this scholarly monograph . . . a writerly text as I hope you shall soon discover.

Preface

There has always been a part-sociological, part-journalistic aspect to my interest in public affairs, and the merging of policy discourse and social practice in this book may have something to do with that predisposition. Also, my disciplinary training and scholarly interest in public affairs most certainly has shaped aspects of the book. Since graduate school, I have often found myself wondering about the differences between policy implementation and public administration as well as their similarities, the separation of public policy from public administration, and the ontological and epistemological presuppositions of public affairs research. Writing papers for and attending conferences, such as the Public Administration Theory Network, Interpretive Policy Analysis, American Society for Public Administration, and the National Communications Association, have given me forums for exploring and learning about new ways to think about public policy and administration. The conception of public administration practice as somehow neutral or objective seems to have lost all its adherents—yet a politics-administration dichotomy remains omnipresent, breathing just in the background, invisibly supplying shared assumptions and predispositions that enable yet delimit numerous conversations. This book tries to get underneath those shared assumptions and predispositions by theorizing anew the "hows" and the "whys" that instigate the accomplishment (or not) of public purposes.

The appendices at the back of the book present illustrative discourses in the areas of drug policy and environmental policy. Unlike industry-specific regulatory agencies, the Environmental Protection Agency (EPA) is broad based, covering numerous forms of industrial pollution. While the EPA is thus less likely to be captured by any single industry, it has seemed that the EPA has spent its entire life in court. The EPA stands as a reminder that public administration is never free from its political environment. Indeed, the administration of natural resources in the United States has been fraught with political turmoil since the early 1900s, as appendix 2 illustrates.

Appendix 1, on drug policy discourse, has a more personal lineage. When I was a college student, an acquaintance of mine failed to return from Kansas to resume his studies after spring break because he had been busted for possession of marijuana. Through the grapevine, I learned that his sentence was to be five years in a state prison. Though I hardly knew him, I was overwhelmed with empathy for the guy. I could not see the point, as an undergraduate student, of yanking a college kid from his studies and sending him instead to a state penitentiary for five years at a cost to the state in excess of $100,000—for possessing under an ounce of cannabis.

The next fall semester, my best essay in my editorial writing class advocated for the legalization of marijuana. Eventually, and by accident, I found a public venue for expressing my irritation; the following summer I was hired as a tennis instructor in Traverse City, Michigan. Taking advantage of a rainy day when tennis classes were canceled, I was running some errands downtown when a newspaper reporter stopped me for a "man-on-the-street" interview. She wanted to know my feelings about Pres. Gerald Ford, a native Michigander himself, being in town. I told the reporter I thought it was great that he was in town for the Cherry Festival but that he really ought to do something useful—such as reverse his predecessor's war on drugs and instead legalize marijuana. Complete with unkempt rainy hair, my picture appeared the next day in the *Traverse City Record-Eagle* with the caption quotation underneath my image: "should legalize marijuana" (Sommerness 1975, 3). Spotting a timely journalistic opportunity, I fired off a well-considered (or so I thought at the time; in retrospect it seems sophomoric) letter to the editor—it was essentially the writing assignment from the previous fall semester—explaining my position on the legalization of marijuana, which was published just a couple days later (Miller 1975). Then, shortly after the letter appeared, I was fired from my tennis-teaching job. This was a big deal. My story was front-page news in the local newspaper (Lynch 1975) and topic of a lead editorial as well ("Coincidence?" 1975), accompanied by a follow-up commentary on free speech, complete with references to Voltaire ("I disapprove of what you say, but will defend to the death your right to say it."). I had some supporters in Traverse City as well as East Lansing who were willing to join my cause, but I, eventually, decided not to pursue legal action against the city. Maybe I should have. Instead, the matter has festered at the back of my mind over the years. And the episode has, time and again, left me shaking my head in disbelief about the irrationality of American antidrug policy. How is it that non-rationality has so thoroughly defeated rationality when it comes to drug policy? Writing this book has given me some tentative answers. Drug policy is not coherent in the logical meaning of the term, but there is, nonetheless, an ideographic coherence to the drug policy discourse. Images, values, and symbols are packaged together in ways that cohere.

The modern image of a rational, autonomous, intentional actor is cast into doubt in narrative analysis, displaced by a decentered subject whose personage is inscribed by childhood experiences, family practices, educational background, and many other cultural influences. A side effect of thinking this way is that it becomes easier to appreciate that, in light of different backgrounds, not everyone shares one's own perspective.

To theorize the irrational yet cohering aspect of public policy, the necessary conceptual material is developed in chapter 1 and put in the context of public policy in chapter 2. The semiotic base of the book's narrative theory is explicated in chapter 3. In chapters 4 and 5, the discussion moves toward administration as daily politics, habitual comportments, and performance of narratives. Throughout, I endeavor to link theory to the illustrative case material found in the appendices whenever a theoretical point requires an example or an illustration.

Governing
Narratives

I
Words/Action

Governing Narratives draws from discourse theory for its conceptual precedents. Torgerson (2003, 121–122) wrote adroitly about the implications of framing a thesis in terms of discourse: "By speaking of policy discourse, we begin to frame the policy world in a decisively new way, clearly locating both analysts and citizens in a communicative context that allows the potential for interchange, challenge and mutual learning. . . . To focus attention on policy discourse is to anticipate democratic possibilities—potential changes in the way citizens, as well as experts, might 'talk policy.' "

Torgerson's optimistic prospects for a democratic policy discourse might also evoke a temperate caveat: democratic inputs into the policy process may not reflect the latest policy research. Weiss's (1977) influential article on the enlightenment function of social research made the point that research is often for policy's sake, in that research alters perceptions among policy makers. With a democratic policy discourse, the causal stories of researchers will not be the only narratives allowed into the sphere of influence. The criteria for policy change will not necessarily be grounded in sound research; advocacy groups may instead use values, emotions, reactions, hyperbole, and any number of additional strategies to induce policy change. What policy makers learn, therefore, might be grounded in creationism rather than evolutionary biology; in market fundamentalism rather than climate change research. Sabatier (1988, 132) astutely focused our attention on beliefs: "They involve value priorities, perceptions of important causal relationships, perceptions of world states. . . . Assuming that people get involved in politics at least in part to translate their beliefs into public policy, this ability to map beliefs and policies on the same 'canvas' provides a vehicle for assessing the influence of various actors on public policy over time."

The narrative approach of this book also focuses on beliefs, but ascribes them not to the actors in an advocacy coalition, but incorporates beliefs and values as aspects of a narrative that is competing for dominance in a field occupied by multiple policy narratives. Policy change continues to be a power struggle, but, in the present thesis, the contest is to capture meaning and advance one narrative or another, thus warranting public action. Public action, once it occurs, is not, thereby, the end of political contestation. Instead, every aspect of public policy and administration is imbued with political potential. Administering environmental policy is different from administering social security policy, which are both different from administering foreign policy or the local building code. The aims and values are different in each of these examples. In addition, even the *how* of administration is imbued with political potential. Apparently neutral and objective tactics and techniques of management are themselves contestable, and they can have profound effects on culture and society.

The term *policy implementation* is, in some ways, preferable to the label *public administration*. Policy implementation directs attention to the mission, to the "what," to the enacted public policy that embraced particular purposes, values, and aspirations. As a stage in the policy process, implementation retains a tight connection to the agency's genesis narrative—the winning argument that was endorsed and legitimated, typically through a legislative process. Public administration has not been renamed policy implementation; instead, the term *public management* has gained ascendancy. The effect is to continue to downplay the political, though it's politics all the way down no matter what term is used to effectuate public policy: implementation, management, or administration.

At the implementation/management/administration phase, we are dealing not only with connotative meanings that inhere in policy discourse but necessarily interject into the mix many other kinds of associations as well. There are relations with others in the workplace and relations with political groups that continue to insist on having say-so over how the policy is put into practice. At implementation, there are now objects in the environment that public policy must reckon with—the very management techniques of public administration may be among them. There are perhaps tools of the trade, chemicals in the water, dismal statistics on social conditions, weather disasters, endangered animals, coal-burning furnaces, aggrieved homeowners, the "not in my backyard" syndrome, and regulation-resistant corporate interests that are among the conceivable situational associations that must be taken into account if the policy mission is to be accomplished. There are already tactics and techniques of management ready to expand into a new domain. Newly introduced policy is born into a world not of its own making.

This book integrates public policy and public administration into a thesis about *governing narratives* and how they change. In the early chapters, the book emphasizes connotation, a particular type of symbolic association. The conceptual core of symbolization in this public policy discourse theory is the ideograph. An ideograph is a constellation of connotations capable of generating meaningful coherence, especially when tied together with story lines into a policy narrative. The winning policy narrative becomes institutionalized as the practices, objects, and relationships of policy implementation are brought into the picture. Amid such symbiotic associations, public purposes are performed.

The presuppositions entailed in this thesis differ from the presuppositions of individual-based social research. Drawing from the field of semiotics, the narrative approach focuses on symbolic meanings, connotations, and associations.

I. SYMBOLIC COMMUNICATION

Public policy discourse generates symbolic meaning that sometimes gains traction in the larger culture. At the same time, from that larger culture public policy discourse draws ideographic meaning. It is a two-way street. And, moreover, it is not always possible to discern a boundary line between a conversation that is public policy discourse and one that is not. Symbolic communication makes associations and crosses boundaries without necessarily clearing it with the rules committee. Through discourse—talking and writing about some events, situations, practices, or beliefs—ideographs and story lines can be arrayed into a subjectively coherent (but not necessarily rational) narrative.

The concept *ideograph* will come up time and again in this book. An ideograph is symbolic material that brings into view a constellation of images, emotions, values, understanding, connotations, and facts. An ideograph is a simpler unit of analysis than a policy narrative, which may additionally interject a story line or two and maybe even introduce a thick plot to convey a more general coherence and complex understanding. Yet, the ideograph is plenty complex on its own. The ideograph's complexity derives partly from the associations among its constituent materials of signifier, signified, and sign. But there is more to it than that. The term *ideograph* has shown up in the communications literature before, so we can start with this prior usage and take it from there: "An ideograph is an ordinary-language term found in political discourse. It is a high-order abstraction representing collective commitment to a particular but equivocal and ill-defined normative goal. It warrants the use of power, excuses behavior and belief, which might otherwise be perceived as eccentric or antisocial, and guides behavior and belief into channels easily recognized by a community as acceptable and laudable" (McGee 1980, 15).

McGee thus aims his definition of ideograph toward public discourse, configuring ideography to be a constitutive part of political commitments and conceptual associations. Ideographic patterns (embedded in stories and narratives) normalize some vision of the world to justify one action or another, one belief or another, one narrative or another, and one policy or another. This normalization is not an automatic or necessarily smooth process, however. Ideographic normalizing is a political struggle, an attempt to associate ideas, objects, or actions with positive resonance or negative resonance, depending on one's perspective and depending on the situation at hand. McGee's claim that an ideograph warrants the use of power invites us to ponder how this might come about in public policy discourse. We can easily imagine, in the agenda formulation phase of the policy process, an emerging policy debate that draws on symbolic associations—including values and emotions—that help make a policy proposal salient. A policy narrative bolstered by salient ideographs can help move a policy proposal through the enactment phase. The winning narrative then enters the implementation phase, where it forms new associations, with certain tactics and techniques perhaps, to enable social action.

Public administration institutionalizes the winning public policy narrative to the extent that ideography is translated into social action. Social action may then evolve into regularized social practice and second-nature habits. Hence, this book is not only about meaning struggles within public policy discourse; it is also about policy implementation and public administration. Habituated ways do not change easily, but, even in the most staid public agency, habitual practices do not signal the end of politics. The narrative may change yet again, challenging the status quo practices and established meanings. New politics can be generated by new ideas, by new practices, and other challenges to the old ways. At moments of impasse, politics' potential to unsettle taken-for-granted practices and ideas becomes evident, even if the institutionalized narrative has become sedimented in the culture, even as practices become increasingly ritualized and habitual. And habit itself is not politically neutral; it tends to side with tradition and the status quo. Narrative governing is thus a political understanding of public affairs, but it also draws from semiotics and other scholarship on symbolic communication.

II. SIGN, IDEOGRAPH, AND NARRATIVE

A. Sign

Signs signify concepts, not objects, Saussure (1983) informs us. This information cannot be accepted lightly. If we are to reject this insight from Saussure, we are then obligated to talk only about those objects in the immediate vicinity, the stuff we can point to. However, if we accept Saussure's insight, we can talk about bears, pepper mills, and anything else, even when they are not physically present. Hence, on practical grounds it is useful to remember that words signify concepts—and not objects, facts, or reality as such. We will return to this topic in chapter 4 to develop it more thoroughly; for now I will simply emphasize that there is a cost to this practical advantage (of language signifying concepts rather than objects) that empirical researchers must pay. The hope for denotative fixity between word and fact must be abandoned. The breach between reality and the ability of language to directly mirror it makes empirical research problematic to the extent that symbolizations, such as words, indicators, and variables, are (mis)taken for reality itself.

A second basic lesson from communications theory is that signs gather meaning not only from the signifier/signified connection, but also from other signs in the language system. Faith is not doubt. Near is not far. Up is not down. Spoon is not fork or knife. Not only do differences generate meaning, but positive associations also contribute to the meaningfulness of signs. Ice is cold. Fire is hot. Positive and negative associations contribute to the meaning of ideographic formations, which bring feelings and values into the context. "Global warming is bad," for example. *Global warming* evokes emotional responses, values, and intellectual considerations, which is to say that there are connotations. Connotation depends on building and establishing differences and similarities—symbolic associations among feelings, values, and concepts, of both positive and negative valence. Connotation is an integral part of the meaning-building process. Signs that may once have enjoyed a positive denotative linkage with some aspect of reality gather connotative baggage as they become familiar through usage. For example, it would be difficult for the term *DDT,* having entered the connotative realm of environmental ideography in the 1960s, to return to the innocent world of denotative positivism. As signs gather in connotations they also expand meaning. Having briefly acknowledged McGee's conception of ideograph above, the next section expands the meaning of the ideograph, as a sign that is rich in connotation and full of implications for public policy discourse.

B. Ideograph

Ideographic materials from the culture's historical archives and from local context find their way into story lines and arguments; the narrative arrangement of this connotative material expresses a particular perspective in policy discourse. One narrative or another will appropriate signs and symbols, including (and sometimes especially) those replete with emotional and moral resonances. The process of framing begins in earnest with ideography, where connotation abounds.

Are the policy implications of poisoning the *American eagle* with DDT more serious than the policy implications of poisoning the *bald eagle* with same? Does the term *marijuana* convey policy implications that the term *cannabis* or *hemp* does not? The imagery of drug policy is tricky for politicians who might consider challenging the dominant narrative. The "soft-on-drugs" taunt is awaiting any legislator who might not vote in favor of punishing *drug lords, violent criminals, moral degenerates, drug abusers,* and of course, *addicts.* The nom de guerre "war on drugs" is itself an evocative ideograph. The term *war* is an incitement to rally against a common enemy. War promises casualties and costs, and by invoking a moral public purpose, justifies them. In drug policy discourse, the imagery varies from the playfully iconoclastic "BONG HiTS 4 JESUS" to the gravely serious "zero tolerance." In the 2007 Supreme Court case *Morse v. Frederick,* 551 U.S. 393, "zero tolerance," a prominent ideograph of the abstinence narrative (explicated in appendix 1), scored a big win over "BONG HiTS 4 JESUS."

Associations, differences, and identifications signal the connotative scope of an ideograph. One might drink vodka because a billboard commercial symbolized sexy urban nightlife. One might drink beer because it symbolizes the sort of fun-loving solidarity that goes with watching football. Smoking marijuana once symbolized an antiestablishment, anti–Vietnam War, counterculture rebel. LSD might also symbolize countercultural creativity. Taking peyote might be part of a sacred ritual or healing treatment. Similarly, abstaining from smoking marijuana might be motivated by the negative resonance of symbols such as *pot head, doper,* or *fry brain.* Beer drinking might symbolize calories and weight gain. One can refrain from all inebriants because they addle the brain or offend God or they damage the body. All these "reasons" for imbibing (or not) entail symbolic association.

In one story line, there is no cure for drug addiction save abstinence. An addict is a criminal who has no one to blame but himself. In a related story line, criminals are deviants, deserving of punishment, not treatment. If they persist in their deviance, well then, more severe punishment is in order. In yet another story line, Schaler (2002) argues that addiction is a lot like willful commitment and is not necessarily a bad thing—one should avoid commitment to a drug that is bad for you just as one should avoid commitment to a personal relationship that is bad for you. The Mexican politician Luciano Pascoe sees drug users as *consumers,* and certainly not as criminals (Wilkinson 2009). Before the concept of addiction gained traction in the culture, those who used drugs on a regular basis were called habitués. In contrast, the term *addict* emphasizes the dangerous aspects of habitual drug use and implicitly takes a stand against becoming one. Some of the names for a regular user of a recreational drug, connoting different emotions and attitudes, include:

- drug addict
- consumer
- drug abuser
- criminal
- patient
- habitué
- pot head
- fiend
- doper

Ideographic images are integrated into story lines that offer a good fit. The regular user of recreational drugs evokes different images in different narratives. For example, in one narrative the drug addict would receive jail time because drug use is a crime, and in another the drug addict would receive health care therapy because addiction is a disease. Even when the same term, *drug addict,* is used, it has different connotations in different narratives.

C. Narrative

Frames or stereotypes or narratives or mental models can help explain why people sometimes have difficulty accommodating dissonant facts. Cognition necessarily creates this effect. We make sense of things through our built-up conceptual apparatus, which is part reason, part passion, part tradition, part character, part setting, and so on. To deny one has a particular perspective would be to deny that one has a culture or a background. None of us language users adopt a totally impartial, unbiased, objective view that is narrative free. Public policy discourse, a political contest over symbolizations, brings identities, feelings, and cultural ideography into the picture. Different narratives generate different sets of relevant facts. As appendix 1 illustrates, each drug policy narrative has its own facts and its own knowledge.

Narratives stitch ideographs together through the use of story lines, but this is the least they do. In characterizing a body of recent sociological research, Somers (1994, 613–614) noted that this body of scholarship postulates

that social life is itself storied and that narrative is an ontological condition of social life. Their research is showing us that stories guide action; that people construct identities (however multiple and changing) by locating themselves or being located within a repertoire of emplotted stories; that "experience" is constituted through narratives; that people make sense of what has happened and is happening to them by attempting to assemble or in some way to integrate these happenings within one or more narratives; and that people are guided to act in certain ways, and not others, on the basis of the projections, expectations, and memories derived from a multiplicity but ultimately limited repertoire of available social, public, and cultural narratives.

And for Ospina and Dodge (2005, 153), "Narrative inquiry provides an appropriate method for tapping into 'local knowledges,' multiple voices, and experiences in context." Hummel (1991) vigorously affirmed the importance of narrative in public administration research.

Appendix 1 illustrates how narratives function in drug policy discourse. The nativist narrative in particular seeks to marginalize drug users, on the one hand, and to associate them with already-stigmatized groups on the other. Sometimes this narrative succeeds in expressing an affirmation of the positive values that *we Americans* stand for; at other times the narrative seems to draw lines in the sand between *us* and *them*. Narratives on drug policy contain causal stories and decline stories, some suggesting dire consequences. Some story lines are angry; others are fearful. There are stories of the good old days, stories of heroes and of villains and of innocent victims. There are elite conspiracy stories, blame-the-victim stories, and unspeakable horror stories. Some of the stories deploy metaphors about war; metaphors about epidemics (of methamphetamine use); and story lines about economic conditions (annual cost, jobs lost, size of the industry, amount of acreage). Story lines that enliven the discourse often include moral messages:

- Addiction should be prevented; the best prevention is abstention; prohibition assures abstention.
- Drug use surrenders our economic might and workplace productivity.
- Drug sentencing policy reflects hypocrisy, injustice, and irrationality.
- Drug prohibition tramples on Americans' freedoms.
- Drug users are not like us. They will harm the nation and our values. The addict lives outside the bounds of decent society.
- Illegal drugs are bad for individuals, families, neighborhoods, and society. By eschewing the values and lifestyles of drug users, wholesome social norms are reinforced.
- People going through the pains of addiction, withdrawal, humiliation, and social stigma need healing. Drug addiction should be treated as a public health issue.
- Drug policy should not do more harm than good.

Other story lines amount to analytical observations or policy advocacy:

• Violation of law on a massive scale damages the institution of law.
• Legalizing marijuana, and taxing it, would bring much-needed money into the public treasury.
• Consumers need good information about the harmful side effects of the product they are considering purchasing.
• The beneficiaries of drug war spending like to keep the war on drugs going for purposes of profits, budgets, employment security, and social status.

Which story to believe is the $64,000 question. Can rational analysis uncover the truest narrative of them all?

D. The Elusive Arbiter of Truth

Jones and McBeth (2010) want to demonstrate the falseness of one narrative or another; but this wish for closure on the facts gains limited traction in actual public policy discourse. Facts are romanced for the sake of the narrative. For example, Rachel Carson's (1962) *Silent Spring* was prefaced with a dramatic story of doom and gloom that influenced the interpretation of the data she presented. In an example from the 1920s, the editors of the *Journal of the American Medical Association* complained about the exaggerations of Richard P. Hobson, who claimed at the time that there were one million heroin addicts; that heroin causes crime; that addicts are beasts and monsters who spread disease like medieval vampires; and that drug addiction is more communicable and less curable than leprosy (Bertram et al. 1996, 70). But the medical establishment's demur on grounds of factuality registered no effect on public policy.

On the other hand, environmental policy discourse has honored scientific norms from the beginning of the U.S. Forest Service (see appendix 2). The environmental movement of the 1960s tended toward applied science. When first introduced, DDT established itself as effectively preventing insect-borne diseases, such as typhus and malaria. Hence, its use expanded. It saved lives in military campaigns of World War II. When later research indicated that fish and birds were dying as a result of pesticide ingestion, the obvious implication was to ban DDT, which eventually transpired despite protests from companies profiting from its sale.

Environmentalism has affected the categories, causal assumptions, and standards of proof used in scientific research (Tesh 2000). In testing a research hypothesis (for example, that a suspected toxin causes a particular disease), the scientific norm has been to reject the null hypotheses (that there is no relationship between the toxin and the disease) only if there is a 5 percent probability or less that the relationship could have occurred by chance. But environmental science is not only about rigor in claim making; its public policy implications have much to do with preventing exposure to harmful substances. The burden of risk is borne by the victims when false negatives are passively endorsed by high-threshold scientific requirements for statistical significance. Terrorist threats do not require that level of certainty before intervention is warranted. *Policy science,* the ideograph, offers hope that false public policy hypotheses can be disproven and dispensed with. No doubt, policy discourse sometimes works that way in narrow technical policy arenas. But scientific rationality in public policy discourse also can be deployed as a political strategy and quite often this is how "science" is used. "In disinterested politics, citizens present their claims as though the claims were free from selfish interests or personal investments. All that counts they say (or imply) are the facts, established by objective scientific research and presented without bias" (Tesh 2000, 100). Science has long grappled with this intractable and recurring problem in its practices, and scientific institutions have established norms of collegial review, replication of research projects, and logical argumentation.

In policy discourse, however, science functions as a connotative ideograph, deployed rhetorically in policy tropes such as "science tells us" or "we have the science on our side." Those engaged in public policy may, with Jones and McBeth (2010), wish for a refuge from the systematic bias, advocacy, manipulation, and gaming that takes place in political environments, a wish no doubt shared by the vast majority of scholars and scientists. But even seemingly objective findings are usually contestable for one methodological reason or another. In terms of policy efficacy, science may or may not serve any given environmental narrative, such as *climate change;* the disinterested posture of scientific ideography may or may not effectively push the policy narrative along. Instead of wishing it were otherwise, this book can be read as an investigation of why science, logic, and rationality are not necessarily trump in public policy discourse. Policy narratives that are not necessarily rational have, time and again, been enacted into law and implemented—while rational solutions have frequently been blocked.

III. SOCIAL ACTION

Legislative enactment legitimates the winning narrative of the discourse that took place in what is often referred to as the agenda formulation phase. Legislative legitimation (enactment) is merely one way among many of enacting social change. There are other ways of enacting change that can also be conceptualized as social action. Organizational subcultures adopt new practices; new technology can change societal practices. Information technology, in particular, can hasten changes in various discourses across the culture, which may affect different practices in different ways. Change is not inevitable; counselors are often frustrated that family systems rarely change their discourses and adopt new practices, though sometimes they do.

The common component in changing societal practices is that ideas, as advanced via ideography and narratives, are enacted and manifested in social action. Hajer (2005) points out that the link between discourse and practice is secured when a narrative or framework gets repeated often enough that it eventually comes to inform the day-to-day meaning system of the policy actors involved. Eventually, a winning narrative dominates and becomes institutionalized into normal social practice (that is, implemented). The ingredients of societal change include not only narrative but also performance. Performance can both challenge established practice and, subsequently, sustain it.

Performance, a concept to be developed in chapter 5, is akin to the concept of social action. Weber's (1978) orientations to social action included: traditional, affectual, value rational, and instrumentally rational. Weber considered, but then steered clear of, the category *imitation,* as it did not jibe with his ontological presupposition of an autonomous, purposive individual. Presupposing instead a decentered subject (which I will describe momentarily), I include in my thesis the category Weber eschewed: imitation. The other precursors to performance discussed below contain recognizable Weberian origins but are adapted to accord with the conceptual framework of the present book, which presupposes not the strong individualism inherent in Weber's work but the decentered subject of poststructuralist thought. The next five subsections each describe analytical categories of performance.

A. Performance from Imitation

Gone viral means that an idea or fashion spreads like a contagion. Ideographic symbols can do this: welfare queen, acid rain, drug lord, and flood of immigrants are symbols that have raced through American hyperreality. Sometimes purposeful intent drives imitation, as when public agencies intentionally attempt to mimic "best practices." Gabriel Tarde (1903) may have been the first scholar to theorize imitation. He thought of imitation as the preeminent social inspiration, as the rule rather than the exception—invention being the exception. As more recent researchers have demonstrated, children learn through imitation, to the point of overimitation. "A phenomenon that we term *overimitation* illustrates a seeming cost of our imitative prowess. Children have been observed to overimitate, or to reproduce an adult's obviously irrelevant actions in several different contexts—even in situations where chimpanzees correctly ignored the unnecessary steps" (Lyons, Young, and Kell 2007, 19751).

Absolute fidelity to the mimicked model is logically possible. However, in practice, mimicking takes place in a social context where the template is only approximated. In organizations, regularized discipline would be expected to lead to high accuracy in the repetition of the ritual. Informal mimicking outside a disciplined setting is subject to numerous contextual suggestions that may inhibit accurate mimicking. Consider forest fire prevention practices. Think of imitation here as fidelity to the formal guidelines. But forest fire prevention in Arizona takes into account a different environment from that of Virginia. There would be little basis for predicting ahead of time whether or not the practice will be accurately replicated in both places; yet, we can still think of the effort to replicate a ritual or a practice as a form of imitation. Custom imitation, fashion imitation, sympathy imitation, obedience imitation, precept imitation, education imitation, naïve imitation, and deliberate imitation are all designated by Tarde (1903) as various iterations of *imitative repetition.*

B. Performance from Feelings

Happiness, guilt, sadness, embarrassment, anger, and many other feelings can inspire actors to behave this way or that way. To the extent that emotions are culturally informed, they are activated by symbolizations such as those communicated in public policy ideography and narratives. Symbolic depictions of cannabis smokers as foreigners (see appendix 1) brought emotional resonance into one of the narratives. Playing to fears of marijuana smokers as rapists and axe murderers, as Harry Anslinger (of the Bureau of Narcotics) did in the 1930s, was another strategic move on the emotional front.

Emotions can come into play even without deliberate manipulation. Sympathy for the forest rangers who died in the Big Burn of 1910 (Egan 2009) generated empathic support for the still-fragile U.S. Forest Service. Meanwhile, once social actors identify with narratives of recycling or energy conservation, emotions such as guilt motivate action and change practice. There are obvious emotional connotations in policy phrases such as *no child left behind* or *freedom to farm*—emotional sparks that have the potential to spur people to social action.

C. Performance from Values

For John Muir, the environmental ethic of preservation of nature for its own inherent value was pursued without the compromising instrumentalism that allowed the construction of a dam in Hetch Hetchy Valley (see appendix 2). As Weber (1978, 25) said of the relationship of the value-rational orientation to social action, it is reflected in the actions of persons "who, regardless of possible cost to themselves, act to put into practice their convictions of what seems to them to be required by duty, honor, the pursuit of beauty, a religious call, personal loyalty, or the importance of some 'cause' no matter in what it consists."

The Sagebrush Rebels (see appendix 2) placed high value on small government, a value orientation that helped inspire the movement's mobilization—even though that value was eventually displaced by a different one (privatization) back at headquarters when the promarket, antigovernment narrative of the Reagan administration gained ascendance in Washington, D.C. (Cawley 1993; see also Somers 2008 for an articulation of the market fundamentalism narrative).

Drug policy discourse, rife with competing value orientations, offers libertarianism and personal freedom in one narrative, while in another offers nativism and prison time for violating laws covering recreational drugs. Meanwhile, values such as harm reduction, industrial productivity, and public safety find expression in other narratives, as explicated in appendix 1. Different narratives express different values.

D. Performance from Instrumentalism

The means-ends calculation that characterizes this action orientation entails rational consideration of alternative means to the end. The end may be determined by fidelity to a particular value, in which case action is instrumentally rational only with respect to the means, according to Weber (1978, 26). Otherwise (and more typically), ends too can be rationally ranked, prioritized, and subject to rational calculation. Economically oriented business activity is perhaps the exemplar in this category, though the literature of political science also tends to presuppose an instrumentally rational orientation toward social action.

Resistance from timber barons and mining companies to the establishment of the U.S. Forest Service was instrumentally rational, at least from their perspective. An unregulated forest was easier to exploit (see appendix 2).

E. Performance from Habit

There comes a time when social action has become regularized, when a way of doing things is done without much conscious thought. The performance of social action reinforces tradition and habit, reinforces regularized practice. This type of performance typically affirms established practices and social order. Importantly, regularized practice makes one predictable to others, a necessary ingredient in cooperative social endeavors. Habit, by definition, does not take hold in the early stages of policy implementation but rather implies regularized practices that have endured over time. Time eventually enables tradition to mask its contestable content. We will return to this topic of habit—and habitus—in chapter 4. The urgent task of the next section is to describe the decentered subject that displaces Weber's intentionally purposive individual.

IV. THE DECENTERED SUBJECT

Redescribing the individual in ideographic terms relies on connotation. In particular, *individual* is itself a connotative ideograph, often taken to be a sovereign, self-determining agent. For Weber and other modernists, the individual is autonomous and independent of others in respect to preferences, values, and goals. In contrast, Mead (1967) posited an individual in relation to other individuals— other individuals being part of the essential, foundational, self-defining, identity-forming component of individuality. The narrative approach goes further than Mead by theorizing the individual as a decentered subject, as poststructuralist philosophy has done.

The autonomy of the individual has been questioned before in interesting ways. Hastings (1998) alleges an *imagined autonomy*. "It is precisely because the reader is required to supply connections or to *work* at making sense of a piece of discourse that they come to believe themselves to be an autonomous individual, a 'subject' which is prior to ideology" (203, emphasis in original). This imagined autonomy, if I read Hastings aright, derives from the cohesive relations in the text that cue the reader as to how to make sense of the text and also recruits the reader into sustaining the narrative. Taking the next step, this book's narrative approach credits ideography, story lines, and narratives with providing the text's cohesive relations, thus displacing the autonomous individual as the site of cohesion. Ideography problematizes the hermetically sealed individual as the social-scientific unit of analysis; but so, too, does statistical research. Statistics has already vanquished the *subject* of most of its individuality. The individual in a database is merely a "record," a row upon which variables, the important stuff in the columns, manifest themselves. The decentered subject, in a strangely similar way, is constituted by social constructions (gathered into ideographs and narratives) that are assimilated by each personage (each row) in unique combinations. Free will, autonomy, and self-interest, usually considered to be attributes of the individual, are, in the narrative approach, ideographs available in the culture's stock of imprints. The decentered subject is a product of the inscriptions accumulated through socialization and experience, by cultural symbolization, and by genetic inheritance.

The unified intentional individual has a place in the brain where there is no further internal dialogue, no contradictions between impulses and logic. All such contradictions have been either worked out or stabilized in the essence of one's personage, where the internal boss presides.

Imagine instead a plurality of places in the brain urging action. The amygdala processes emotional reaction, the thalamus regulates awareness, and the putamen regulates movements. As Sigmund Freud would say, the ego is not master in its own house. One conscious thought wants to take exception to what was just said. Another impulse wants peaceful coexistence more than an argument. A third place in the brain remembers something from the past that feels like the current situation. Meanwhile, the amygdala monitors the existential present and injects an emotional fight/flight dimension into the mix. In different situations, one can express a variety of competencies, concepts, associations, norms, rationales, and so on that one's thinking brain has entertained, considered, selected, deselected, remembered. To the extent that any personal tendencies are dominant, such tendencies have consistent say-so over one's ethics and one's judgments about appropriate behavior.

For a decentered subject, the concept of *self* functions as a sort of clearinghouse, or gatekeeper—a switchman rather than the boss. The decentered subject develops across generations as the culture and language have developed and as genes have evolved. This notion that the human subject is constituted by cultural practices is a stark departure from the conception of society as a loosely connected gathering of free autonomous individuals. Inscriptions—from family background, educational influences, socialization, acculturation, media messages from magazines, radio, television, and the Internet—compose the persona. "We derive a sense of 'self' from drawing upon conventional, pre-existing repertoires of signs and codes which we did not ourselves create. We are thus the *subjects* of our sign-systems rather than being simply instrumental 'users' who are fully in control of them" (Chandler 2002, 218). Which of the historically built-up concepts, norms, and practices that have been selected into the personage are relevant at any particular time is not known in advance. Yet, at the moment of performance, one selects from among the ideographs that inform the context. Most likely, I will do what I have done before, though maybe not this time.

A decentered subject is not an already-existing, preconstituted entity, as the autonomous individual of the Enlightenment tends to be portrayed, but a subject constituted by and through associations—relationships with others in society and interactions with social practices, physical objects, and cultural symbols. Subjects are associational and relational entities that both establish themselves and change themselves over time; they take action as embodied sets of roles, expectations, ways, practices, and norms that have been inscribed on their various personages over the course of life. With a decentered subject displacing the autonomous individual, the unit of analysis in discourse theory need not be limited to persons who are countable into categories. Instead, we can more readily make use of communicative units of analysis, such as signs, ideographs, and narratives, and link these directly to social action and performance via the decentered subject.

Chapter 1 attempted to provide the reader with some idea of the concepts and theoretical building blocks that will be further developed in the chapters ahead. Chapter 2 begins this work in earnest, by linking communication theory to some of the policy literature that deals with symbolism and social construction.

2
The Mobilization of Stories

The study of public policy has emphasized the importance of communication from its earliest days. Pioneer policy scholar Harold Lasswell, who was also a communication theorist, wrote a book about propaganda. His seminal article in *Policy Sciences* (1970) was attentive to the role of persuasion strategies in the policy process. The literature on policy agenda formulation has been particularly attentive to communication theory. Rochefort and Cobb (1993, 56) argued, "Use of language is critical in determining which aspect of a problem will be examined. Rhetoric can help lodge a particular understanding of a problem in the minds of the public and protagonist." In the present thesis, policy communication is seen as a political contest among competing ideographic narratives on a symbolic playing field. One narrative may rise to dominance when it is legitimated through political processes. A legitimated policy narrative in turn licenses social action, warranting organizational practices such as those found in policy implementation and public administration. The process plays out through various phases of symbolic meaning making.

I. SYMBOLIC POLITICS

Signs, ideographs, and story lines must be constructed *just so* if one's favored interpretation is to prevail over the others. Reason and rationality frame the meaning only in certain conditions, as public policy meaning making often can be a cultural struggle rather than a rational-analytical project. Rational-analytical statements often play out as political claims in public policy discourse. Hallowed traditions venerating "objectivity" advance only a vague cognizance of the political embeddedness of their claims. Stone's (1997) critique of the dominant mode of policy thinking deconstructs rationality as a genre of storytelling.

Policy discourse in general can be thought of as deliberately fashioned portrayals of situations or issues. Examples can be readily imagined. The *inheritance tax* morphed into an *estate tax* and more recently has been named a *death tax* by language-savvy antitax political consultants. Representations of a problem are fashioned to gain leverage and sympathy for a point of view or a policy prescription. Ideographic representations of problematic situations have been used to influence public policy discourse in one direction or another:

• welfare dependency
• career criminals
• serial predator
• drug lord
• choose life
• flood of immigrants
• smokers' rights
• a liberal
• death panel
• leave no child behind
• three strikes and you're out
• drug addict

A narrative approach would seek to get beneath, around, and behind the way the media, society, lobbyists, public relations consultants, and people in government discuss public policy. The affectations of objectivity and neutrality will probably not be abandoned in policy analysis any time soon, if only because "objective facts" are often effective trump cards played by one advocate or another; this device works in any number of narratives. But the problem is something much deeper than an unacceptable neglect of the political (Stone 1997). The problem with objective facts is not only that they are invoked in a strategic way, but also that the sought-after, one-to-one correspondence between words and facts, typically presupposed in the protocols of empirical research, cannot be had. Wittgenstein (2009) argued that we must, therefore, settle for local "language games" in which the meaning of words depends on the setting and the participants. With Wittgenstein, a narrative approach also refuses the presupposition that every word has a meaning that corresponds to its object. The implications of this disconnect from word and object casts doubt not only on the rationality project. The gap between word and fact makes problematic the denotative connection between reality and social science research methods in general, both quantitative and qualitative. In a narrative approach, words are rarely precise in their denotative meaning, and instead connote different things in different contexts. The unrecoverable gap between a word and the object it purports to represent cannot be completely traversed by language, mathematics, or any system of symbolic representation.

The velocity of information flowing through society, including the Internet, further inhibits social researchers' efforts to denote straightforward facts. Information exchange has accelerated beyond what was imaginable in the print era or even the television era. Symbolic expressions, sometimes charged with meaning, energy, or emotion, arouse attention. Sometimes information bits circulating in social space (virtual or otherwise) disrupt stable narratives and coherent sense making. Other times the circulation of signs allows them to connect to other signs in unanticipated ways, generating new meaning. Signs may link with other signs and images, forming ideographs, which are constellations of signs, images, meanings, and emotions. Those symbols that do not arouse concern of some sort are met with indifference or neglect—the ineffectual cast-offs of linguistic evolution. Wittgenstein's (2009) ideas about the ambiguity, situatedness, and perspectivism of actual language usage underscore the practical ways in which interacting humans reduce the denotative ambiguity of language through training and context. Saussurean semiotics (which will be discussed in chapter 3) enables me to take the residual ambiguity of communication, not as something to be overcome, but as an occasion for thinking differently about the meaning-making process—which turns out to be mostly a connotative rather than denotative process. Language is alive in that its component meanings evolve and change over time.

Ideography plays a large role in public policy struggle for meaning capture, but how this role operates remains unexplored territory in public policy and administration. Though now recognized as a salient phenomenon in the public policy literature, symbolic politics was once mere distraction for dupes. Symbolic benefits would accrue to losers. Perhaps symbols would serve as inspiration during the planning stage of some democratic idealism. A bill would be named "Save the Family Farm" Act, or, later, the "Freedom to Farm" Act. But watch where the resources go and discover that family farms continue to go out of business at the same rate as before, while large agribusiness continues to accrue government farm subsidies at the same rate as before. The inspirational names for legislative bills were thought to be merely symbolic; *who gets what* is the real politics.

Eventually, it seemed there might be more than disingenuous feint to the symbolism of public policy. Edelman (1977; 1988) was an astute early observer of symbolic politics. While his 1977 book sometimes expressed the familiar disdainful attitude toward empty symbols, his 1988 book more fully appreciated symbols for their meaning-generating role, their importance to politics, and their irony. He pointed out that the statement by the U.S. State Department of the 1980s that "El Salvador is protecting human rights" also ironically conveys the reverse possibility: Why is the State Department bothering to defend El Salvador's human rights record? *El Salvador's elites are assailing human rights.* Cobb and Elder (1973) were also among the political scientists to theorize the role of symbolization in the formation and expression of mass political coalitions, wherein symbols gather individual identities and identifications. A focus on "the symbolic nature of social attachments" (Cobb and Elder 1976, 309) offered a viable alternative to the group-based political paradigm. The study of symbolic politics has resulted in greater awareness of the use of clever marketing, dubious manipulation, and political spin. Some maneuvers seem clever and justifiable to their supporters, perhaps deceitful and scheming from other ideological standpoints. Yet, it becomes possible, perhaps with some effort, to study the use of manipulative symbolic imagery in a dispassionate way. The baseball analogy "three strikes and you're out" was used to the effect of increasing the prison population in the United States; astonishment over this phenomenon eventually yields to a more distanced appreciation of the art of symbolic manipulation. Those who wanted to crack down on repeat criminals recruited the baseball metaphor "three strikes and you're out" to pass legislation that required a life prison sentence for "career criminals" convicted of the third felony and, in doing so, removed a good measure of judicial discretion. "Three strikes and you're out" is what older siblings and the older kids in the neighborhood had to tell the younger playmate who had just struck out but wanted to continue at bat and have another chance to hit the ball. This was often a very tough rule for a youngster to learn—you only get three swings at the ball. If you can't hit it after trying three times, you are "out" and not allowed to swing at any more pitches until your time at bat cycles around again. So, "three strikes and you're out" was imported into the policy discourse as a way of sending repeat offenders to prison for the rest of their lives. While not logically coherent, the baseball metaphor worked magnificently to give a get-tough, antidrug, and anticrime policy some narrative coherence. "Three strikes and you're out" legislation became law as the baseball metaphor was appropriated into the service of public policy discourse and was implemented to profound effect on the lives of those caught with illegal drugs for the third time.

Once attuned to noticing that cultural metaphors can mutate into public policy symbols, their presence seems ubiquitous. American presidential campaigns generate some of the most vivid imagery: compassionate conservatism; a thousand points of light; morning in America; change we can believe in. Even if campaign symbols become meaningless in the long run, in the short run it apparently benefits a political candidate to associate herself with positive images, dissociate from negative images, and plaster one's opponent with negative associations.

Importing slogans into public policy debates helps to frame the issue in a particular way. If "it takes a village to raise a child," then feeding and caring for children must be a public responsibility. If cocaine addicts have children who are "crack babies," then we need to ratchet up the war on drugs and worry less about social services. If we want to have the "freedom to farm," then we will surely want to cut government farm subsidies. If one wants to restrict the sale of guns, then regulating ammunition, especially "cop-killer bullets," would be a good place to start. By redescribing the medical procedure "intact dilation and evacuation" as "partial birth abortion," religious conservatives created a powerful symbolic weapon in the struggle to redefine human life and recriminalize abortion in the United States. Story lines bring additional power of persuasion to ideographic images and create new or different understanding of appropriate policy action. We typically change the way we talk and think about an issue before we change public policy about it, although Weick (1979) would remind us that rationalization for action can come after the fact. Because symbolization has direct links to social practices, a narrative approach takes symbolization into its account of the policy process. Even scientific and highly technical policy debates are, paradoxically, hammered out in policy arenas that are often "highly resistant to resolution by appeal to evidence, research, or reasoned argument" (Schön and Rein 1994, xi). The norms of science and rationality that have informed public policy research have also hidden from view those vexing aspects of public policy discourse that slip the grip of methodological rigor and empirically verifiable causality.

II. POLITICS AND EPISTEMOLOGY

Images, ideology, and cultural presuppositions express ideographic units of analysis; an ideographic unit of analysis differs from the individual unit of analysis presupposed in most treatises in the fields of public policy and administration. This book's narrative approach analyzes signs, ideography, and language rather than individuals or aggregations of them such as group, organization, or political unit. Certain unique challenges arise because of this. When social scientists presuppose the individual as the unit of analysis, the concept of social actor appears to be fairly straightforward. How can social action transpire if the unit of analysis is a symbolization of some sort? To put the answer briefly, symbolic understanding translates into action through the decentered subject. The decentered subject is a personage composed of historically accumulated cultural inscriptions as well as genetic traits. Signs develop significance and meaning as they are gathered together in association with one another into ideographs, which then may organize into policy-relevant story lines to become dominant narratives that are enacted into practice through social action. Human agency eventually translates discourse into social action through the meaningful performance of such associations. At each stage of the process, it could have been otherwise. That is, this process of symbol replication and connotative association could either support or sabotage a developing narrative and, hence, the performance of social action.

Ideas such as replication and connotative association may seem jarring and perhaps incomprehensible from a traditional policy science perspective. But over the years the traditional positivist paradigm has been found wanting among critical policy scholars who have turned to interpretive approaches.

A. Interpretive Approaches

Western science has brought disciplined research methods to bear on natural phenomena. The rigorous approach of science has yielded historic achievements. On several occasions, science has revealed religious modes of interpretation as lacking coherence and evidence. Galileo's experiments with the telescope and Darwin's theory of evolution are the seminal examples. The professional skepticism of science should also characterize policy science, one might reasonably argue. Indeed, the mainstream of public policy thought supposes that policy analysts will retain scholarly norms when it comes to argumentation and reason giving. But in applying scientific norms to policy analysis, researchers can easily overestimate the ability of social indicators to represent social reality. In her acclaimed critique of the performance movement in public administration, Radin (2006, 236) concluded that, contrary to the classic assumptions of performance assessment, "It is important that individuals involved with performance measurement think about the symbolic meanings that are attached to programs and policies" and to see issues as others see them.

If such symbolic consciousness is recommended for the evaluation phase of the policy process, it may well apply in all phases of the policy process. But Radin's essay on performance accountability scarcely scratched the surface of symbolic meaning. Hermeneutics, poststructuralism, Lacanian psychoanalysis, critical management studies, and discourse analysis informed the approach of Glynos (2008) and Glynos and Howarth (2007). They lay out three policy logics relevant for understanding symbolic meaning in the policy process. Their typology—the logic of social practice, political logic, and fantasmatic logic—shows how the interaction between symbolization and policy practice unfolds. For their framework, institutionalized social practices are a way of quelling anxiety, and "the role of fantasy is to actively contain or suppress the political dimension of a practice. Thus, aspects of a social practice may seek to maintain existing social structures by preemptively absorbing dislocations, preventing them from becoming the source of a political practice. In fact, the function of many management and governance techniques could be seen in this light" (Glynos and Howarth 2007, 146). Fantasy thus possesses conservative potential because institutional symbolization can be deployed to prevent potential challenges to the status quo from even registering the distress that would-be change agents may be experiencing. Glynos (2008, 275) admitted that "it may seem odd to link fantasy with work," but peoples' fantasies have the power to "structure the motivations underpinning much economic practice, production practices included."

Lacanian psychoanalysis, hermeneutics, and critical theory may seem exotic forms of policy science, but the attempt to mimic scientific methods in practical social settings can easily miss the larger social-political background. Critics contend that the consequence of the positivist style of policy analysis is to advance unwelcome technocratic governance. Fischer (e.g., 2003) has long espoused a reframing of policy analysis, emphasizing argumentation and discourse in public policy processes. First, says Fischer, we should recognize the importance of values and how they are conveyed in narrative storytelling about policy problems. Talking about values expands the discussable range of a policy problem. Expanding the realm for communication and argumentation can be thought of as a form of public enlightenment. Majone (1992, 1) endorsed this line of thinking: "As politicians know only too well but social scientists too often forget, public policy is made of language. Whether in written or oral form, argument is central in all stages of the policy process." At the very least, empirical-causal-technicist policy analysis is but one approach among many possible and credible approaches to policy analysis. From among them, Fischer (2003) devotes his energies to argumentative and discursive modes to refocus public policy studies on shared social meanings. He advocates a disciplined practice of policy argumentation. "Whereas a narrative ties together a story with a beginning, and middle, and an end through the device of a plot, an argument is structured around premises designed to logically lead to conclusion" (181). Policy analysis, then, functions to tease out the crux of the argument embedded in the story. "While political actors tell stories, it is the argument that constitutes the basic unit of real-world policy analysis" (182). Offering an *argumentative approach* to evaluating policy analysis, Fischer (2003, 183) emphasizes "the context-specific rhetorical character of analytical practices—the ways the symbolism of language matters, the ways the consideration of audiences needs to be taken into account, how solutions depend on problem construction." How the norms of argumentation would play out in practice depends on the context—the policy problem under consideration, its power dynamics, competing values that come into play, the historical moment, and the immediately preceding events. Whereas formal argument takes place within a systematized set of axioms and rules of inference, "practical argumentation starts from opinions, values, or contestable viewpoints rather than axioms" (190). Hence, the locus of attention necessarily shifts toward opinions and values expressed in a context. In a later book, Fischer (2009, 193) broadened his thesis to include narrative and emotion as primary considerations as well, seeing a need to "recognize that arguments typically deal with pieces of the larger patterns drawn out by a narrative." Argument may thus be understood as a particular style of story line within a narrative.

As Gottweis (2007) and Fischer (2009) have pointed out, public policy is much more than *logos* (rational discourse). It is also about *pathos* (emotions) and *ethos* (which includes character, ethics, place, and habit). Problem definition may be based on evaluation, evidence, and argumentation, but the norms of problem definition vary according to one's perspective—to include one's perceived interests, one's normative predispositions, and one's cultural background. Beyond the point that public policy often is not rational, the policy analyst must also appreciate that different subcultures have different policy priorities and different policy communities have their own ways of selecting which ideas to advance or ignore. Narratives are advanced to reflect these different perspectives and experiences. Ideographs, symbols, and meanings can easily hitchhike on a media-fed informational cascade based on a bandwagon effect. The formation of narratives can derive, not only from historically embedded cultural practices or strategic manipulation, but also from chance encounters with fleeting symbolic imagery.

B. No Solution, No Problem

If public policy worked like science, we could apply Program A (the independent variable) to Problem 22 (dependent variable), and Problem 22 would go away or its symptoms would disappear, just as taking a painkiller, such as aspirin, might solve the problem of a headache. But in public policy discourse, causality functions differently. "Cause" is part of the narrative that frames the issue. For example, observations of bacteria and protozoa along with a contagion theory of disease were known, or at least hypothesized, as early as the 16th century. Nowadays, this theory explains how people catch colds and the flu and is widely accepted. But it had a rough start. Despite the causal power of the contagion explanation of disease, ideas about contagion remained dubious well into Britain's

19th century (Tesh 1988). Contagion theory was politically unpalatable among the industrialists and traders of sea-faring Britain. The policy implication of the contagion theory of germs entailed the possible quarantine of people and the closing of ports. "It was impossible to separate the scientific debate about disease causality from the economic consequences of its application" (Tesh 1988, 15). In other words: *no solution, no problem.* As there was no causal narrative that could achieve an acceptable closure, there was no policy. Wildavsky (1987, 26) elaborates, "A problem in policy analysis, then, cannot exist apart from a proposed solution, and its solution is part of an organization, a structure of incentives without which there can be no will to act." And eventually a fully complete causal narrative regarding the spread of disease came into ascendancy. Near the end of the 19th century, the contagion theory of germs made a comeback. This time, the solution to contagion did not necessarily involve closing the ports because by the late 1800s vaccines and antibiotics were available. "Carrying with it this time the possibility of antibiotics and vaccines to control diseases without the threat of quarantine, the theory rapidly overtook other explanations for disease" (36). The causal relationship between bacteria and disease thus became accepted.

C. Causal Stories

The question of causality opened a fault line between what Fischer (2003) describes as empirical-analytical social science, on one hand, and interpretive theory on the other. "While empiricist social scientists stress the analysis of cause-effect relationships, they seldom establish any such relationship. Empirical analysts generally uncover statistical correlations between events, but are unable to prove that one caused the other (that is, that A appeared before B and thus made B happen)" (158). Fischer does not therefore dismiss quantitative empirical-analytical research as useless—such research often does say something about the variables involved and the direction in which they move. But he, nonetheless, makes a strong claim: "Only through interpretive methods can we discover the various possible explanations of what particular actors thought they were doing when they engaged in the actions pertinent to the causal relationships" (158).

Rather than look for the foundations on which to base a causal chain, Stone (1997) let go of the idea of causal foundation as a truth-proving endeavor and instead appreciated causality as a particular kind of story line used to rearrange alliances and do persuasive work in policy communities. "We often think we have defined a problem when we have described its causes. Policy debate is dominated by the notion that to solve a problem, one must find its root cause or causes; treating the symptoms is not enough" (188). Speaking in terms of causes not only references the imagery of careful scientific research, but once a "true" cause establishes itself, all the other theorized causes can be dismissed. Hence, causality belongs not only to rigorous research but also to the realm of politics and storytelling. Causes tend to assign responsibility for problems, which often entails blaming one group or another for causing the problem. Finding a cause often means finding a victim, a perpetrator, and a workable narrative. Causal stories are crafted strategically, using symbols and categories of things to count. These stories shape alliances and affect policy choices, with the subsequent effects on society and target groups within it. In the drug policy narratives presented in appendix 1, causal stories frame the understanding of the situation in one particular way or another, and the differences among these causal stories are telling:

• Overuse of narcotics causes addiction.
• Drug addiction ruins lives.
• Smoking marijuana causes violent behavior, murder, and rape.
• Illegality of drugs leads to obscene profits for drug dealers, misallocation of resources, and civil rights violations.
• Intolerance of the other (that is, bigotry and racism) causes the war on drugs.
• Drug and alcohol use causes workplace accidents and decreased productivity.
• Entrenched economic interests (the drug war enforcement complex) cause the government to continue with a failed policy.
• Forcing markets underground leads to police corruption and organized gang violence.

In Stone's typology, some causes are both unguided and unintended—accidents of nature or perhaps malfunctioning machines. When one is charged with responsibility for disastrous consequences, the "accidental causality" story line might be proffered in defense: These things happen; it's nobody's fault. Proponents of free markets and deregulation emphasize the "unintended consequences" story line in discussing policies such as rent control, minimum-wage laws, and welfare programs. Unintended consequences might include driving landlords out of the market, increasing the costs of hiring, and creating disincentives to find work. Blaming computer error would be another type of causal story, one that embraces a mechanical explanation. Mechanical explanations can easily become as complex as the technological systems that undergird them, but the theme is that, although there were worthy purposes intended, the system behaves as if intervening agents perform unguided actions, generating dysfunctions and displaced objectives. A system designed to end hunger may, in its operation, increase the incidence of diabetes. However, if one is on the offense, story lines replete with intentional causes can be powerful. Oppression of the poor by the elite, conspiracies among the insiders, and continuation of harmful programs point toward willful human action by guilty perpetrators. Tobacco companies played into this story line when they obfuscated findings about tobacco's detrimental health effects and addictive qualities (*New York Times* 1994). If the causal consequence is good rather than bad, the story line's causal chain is linked back to rational and competent leadership and public policy implementation.

Stone's deconstruction of causal stories exposes unexamined metaphysical presuppositions embedded in policy discourse; these presuppositions often can be dogmatic assertions that entail underappreciated complications. She shows that policy arguments are undergirded by rhetorical maneuvers; that even supposedly neutral analytical statements contain political claims. So far, so good; but the strategic representation of causal relations is only one way that policy narratives are socially constructed.

III. SYMBOLIC SOCIAL CONSTRUCTION

In their oft-cited article, Schneider and Ingram (1993) described metaphorical representation as an instance of *social construction*. They were particularly interested in the social construction of *target populations* when they wrote: "The social construction of target populations refers to the cultural characterizations or popular images of the persons or groups whose behavior and well-being are affected by public policy. These characterizations are normative and evaluative, portraying groups in positive or negative terms through symbolic language, metaphors, and stories" (334).

Their article was soon denounced as lacking in clear causal argument (Lieberman 1995). Ingram and Schneider (1995, 442) responded, "In our theory of causation, motivations of elected officials are linked to the types of policy designs they construct, which affect people's experiences with the policy and the lessons and messages they take from it." Policy designs have their own subsequent effects, influencing values, attitudes, and group identities in the polity as well as political participation and attitudes toward government. Their 2005 anthology, *Deserving and Entitled*, contained multiple case studies showing how some groups were marginalized by the way they were constructed in public policy discourse, while other groups were embraced as both deserving and entitled. Appreciative that the principle of equality is deeply ingrained in American consciousness, Schneider and Ingram (2005, 2) credit public policy for legitimating, extending, and creating distinctive populations, while, at the same time, noting that some are extolled as deserving and others excluded as ineligible. Suffrage laws extended the right to vote to new populations, while, at the same time, they deprived others. Veterans, a deserving group, continue to enjoy advantages in federal civil service practices. The changing social construction of Japanese Americans is studied in two of the chapters. Race and poverty provide background conditions for social constructions of undeserving populations; immigration and welfare policy discourses construct additional deserving and undeserving target populations. The drug policy discourse presented in appendix 1 illustrates how target populations are constructed in that discourse, and the next section is a reflection on one of those constructions.

A. Social Construction of Drug War Target Populations

Creating a rationale for U.S. drug policy entailed the construction of a target population (Schneider and Ingram 1993). Sometimes the construction of the target population was aimed directly at drug users. "We intend to get the killer-pushers and their willing customers out of selling and buying dangerous drugs. The answer to the problem is simple—get rid of drugs, pushers, and users. Period" (Harry Anslinger of the 1930s-era Bureau of Narcotics, quoted in Krebs 1975). But more often drug users were associated with socially vulnerable groups, serving to further marginalize both drug users and ethnic minorities.

Curiously, the term *marijuana* was not well known before the 1930s. The physician Horatio Wood (1869) described his experiments with cannabis grown in Lexington, Kentucky, without using the word marijuana. He concluded, "There can be no doubt that under certain circumstances cannabis indica supplies a medical mood, which no other drug will so exactly meet" (231). The *New York Times* (1926b) named the drug "cigarettes made of the leaves of the cannabis indica," "canjac," and "hashish," even though at another point in the story hashish was identified as an incorrect reference. The headline contained the words *marijuana, hemp,* and *the weed.* "The weed" is "really Indian hemp," the article later noted; or maybe "ganja." But it also might be "cannabis indica or sativa." The association of marijuana with Mexicans had strategically expanded by 1935, with the Federal Bureau of Narcotics (FBN) claiming that "fifty percent of the violent crimes in districts occupied by Mexicans, Spaniards, Latin-Americans, Greeks, or Negroes may be traced to this evil" (Bonnie and Whitebread 1974, 100). Musto (2002) tracked down FBN reports on marijuana from 1931, 1933, and 1937, all titled "Traffic in Opium and Other Dangerous Drugs." The first report, from 1931, merely contrasts Indian hemp and Chinese hemp and when it does mention "marihuana," the word is placed within quotation marks and linked to the Mexican population in the Southwest (423). The 1933 report uses the terms *Indian hemp, cannabis sativa,* and *marijuana* interchangeably and notes that Mexican laborers clandestinely plant it among beet plants (424). The 1937 report is dramatically different. It tells of local eradication programs; it uses the term *marijuana* exclusively; and it names villains' minority ethnic status. For example: "Pete

Lopez, alias Mexican Pete, was growing and selling marijuana. . . . [Officers purchased seven ounces] from him and from a colored woman, Lucy Vaughn" (427). In another passage, "Wong Kop, café operator and prominent member of Memphis's Chinese colony" was sentenced (429). Marijuana was first criminalized in the same year as the 1937 report. The Spanish-language term enabled easy ideographic association between Mexican immigrants and the recreational drug marijuana. The FBN under Harry Anslinger, as well as Hearst newspaper reporters known for their "yellow journalism" style of sensationalism, constructed marijuana users as rapists and killers, as well as Mexican immigrants, immediately before and after the enactment of the Marihuana Tax Act of 1937. In an interview, Anslinger told David F. Musto that his appointment as commissioner of FBN was helped by the crucial support of William Randolph Hearst (Musto 1999, 209). Hearst newspapers were not the only source for screechy marijuana headlines, however. One *New York Times* (1926a) headline read: "Kills Six in a Hospital: Mexican, Crazed by Marijuana, Runs Amuck with Butcher Knife."

The ideography of drug use became conspicuously connotative when cocaine psychosis was linked to black males. Media images of bullet-resistant, cocaine-crazed black men possessed of extraordinary marksman skills accompanied the first regulation of cocaine. In the public debate leading up to the passage of the Harrison Act in 1914, which regulated and taxed narcotics, an M.D. by the name of Edward Huntington Williams wrote a piece for the *New York Times Sunday Magazine* about a new southern menace causing murder and insanity: Negro cocaine fiends. The problem, according to Williams (1914, 12), was that Georgia, North Carolina, South Carolina, Tennessee, and West Virginia "passed laws intended to keep whiskey and the negro separated. These laws do not, and were not intended to, prevent the white man or the well-to-do negro getting his accustomed beverages through legitimate channels." The laws also did away with saloons, "but a large proportion of the intelligent whites were ready to make this sacrifice if by doing so they could eliminate the drunken negro" (12). This astonishing story purports to explain why these southern states have incarcerated so many more insane drug users—the consequent fact seems to be that, after the new laws were passed, lower-class blacks had access to cocaine, but not whiskey, thus creating a criminal race menace fueled by cocaine, in Williams's view. Cocaine fiends are particularly dangerous because, according to Williams, normal bullets don't knock them down as they would a sane man. The chief of police of Asheville, North Carolina, had to increase the caliber of his weapon after the "negro drug fiend" he was trying to kill did not even stagger when hit by a normal bullet. Police officers all over the south "have made a similar exchange for guns of greater shocking power for the express purpose of combating the 'fiend' when he runs amuck." On the other hand, the story continues, cocaine use near Asheville increased the accuracy of the "cocaine nigger [who] dropped five men dead in their tracks, using only one cartridge for each" (Williams 1914, 12).

Chinese immigrants were the target group of the West Coast's early opium laws, as reported in appendix 1. In 1875, San Francisco outlawed the smoking of opium—the first time drugs had been banned in the United States. The association of opium smoking with Chinese immigration "was one of the earliest examples of a powerful theme in the American perception of drugs, that is, linkage between a drug and a feared or rejected group within our society" (Musto 2002, 184–185). The specific content of the marginalized target group has varied over the years, but TraditionalValues.org (2009) carries on the tradition in an article titled "Barney Frank Wants America to Be Woodstock Nation." According to the article, "Massachusetts gay activist Barney Frank (D) not only wants to force all Americans to affirm the lifestyles of gays, lesbians, bisexuals, drag queens, and transsexuals, but he also wants us to get high on marijuana, too." Harsh drug policy is an opportunity to express disdain for deviance; it connotes a willingness to confront the difficult-to-control elements of society who have already demonstrated, by nonconventional drug choices, a willingness to eschew mainstream orthodoxy. An efficient mechanism for pressuring recalcitrant individuals, drug policy also functions to stabilize the status quo by exorcising from the political community counterculture threats. As drug policy became a war on drugs, the culture war against "the other" intensified.

The causal associations of marijuana with rape, murder, and suicide were not credible in the long run. Demonization of drug users was perhaps an effective strategy in articulating the dominant drug policy narrative, nonetheless. Endemic to the narrative was the theme of otherization, wherein drug users were framed as different, and not just in terms of their choice of recreational drug. They were presented as if from a different nationality or subculture. Their values were not wholesome, patriotic American values.

Such ethnic associations were effective in connoting *other*. Opium connoted Chinese immigrants; cocaine connoted murderous black men; marijuana connoted evil Mexicans and, later, the war-protesting Woodstock nation. The connotations often elicited emotions of disgust or fear among the general population. At its nastiest, this nativist narrative generates and reinforces racial and ethnic stereotypes and warrants extreme incarceration. At its best, the nativist narrative functions to assist culture in determining who is *us* and who is *them*. What do we stand for? What should our practices consist of? What are our common values? Social cohesion depends, to some extent, on a common answer to these sorts of questions. But the nativist narrative also carries with it the possibility of an unjust stigmatizing. It may signal societal irresolution that needs serious attention, as when a normalized mainstream privileges itself against deviant others. The exteriorization that results from these practices has consequences that go deep into cultural identities. Exclusions, such as occurred during the witch craze (Oplinger 1990), the Palmer Raids, and the Holocaust, function to reinforce the identity of the normal people. Laclau (2005, 70) offers the general template for this thesis: "So . . . the only possibility of having a true outside would be that the outside is not simply one more neutral element but an *excluded* one, something that the totality expels from itself in order to constitute itself (to give a political example: it is through the demonization of a section of the population that a society reaches a sense of its own cohesion)."

When drug policy functions as an *otherizing* technique, the politics can be seen as a clash between status quo normalcy seeking to preserve its orthodoxy and a not-yet-mainstream cultural tendency that poses a heretical challenge. Orthodoxy's *fulsome whole* is affirmed when the excluded elements function to reinforce the identity of the whole population. For example, illegal immigrants, through their exclusion, provide the whole of the native population its identity. But if the exclusion harms the fulsome whole of society, which now might have to reconcile itself to its own bigotry and prejudice, the exclusion functions quite differently. The fulsome whole is undermined when groups that should be part of "us" are turned away as "them"—are *otherized*. Otherization undermines the fulsome whole when subparts of the population are wrongly exteriorized.

For those opposed to locking up recreational drug users, their exclusion signifies a compelling and shared absence, a wound to the fulsome whole. *Otherization* would in this sense function as a signifier of loss and ache, directing attention toward the immanent injustice of exclusion through incarceration and other forms of sanction and humiliation.

Meanwhile, drug users and illegal immigrants (to take but two groups who, at this writing, are stigmatized) are dealt with according to the rules of dispatch—prison and/or deportation. There is no harmonizing their struggle with other struggles of ostracized people, as happened in the civil rights movement. A sympathetic moment came in 2009 when the sentencing disparities between crack cocaine and powder cocaine were acknowledged as racist in the United States. Mostly, however, for both drug users and illegal immigrants, there is no discursive traction for joining the struggle of "the people," no access to the fulsome whole, little opportunity to have their exclusion politicized. Instead, exteriorizing keeps illegal immigrants and drug users alike out of decent society's self-definition, as exemplars of *not-us*.

Drug policy discourse constructed target populations to fit the narratives, but rationality, and especially science, were not integral to the discourse. In the drug policy debate, scientific findings were typically subordinated to an obvious policy agenda. Regarding the official annual statistical report, *National Drug Control Strategy,* published by the U.S. Office of National Drug Control Policy (ONDCP), Robinson and Scherlen (2007, xiv-xv) surmise that either: "(1) ONDCP knowingly uses statistics to mislead about the drug war; or (2) the authors of its annual Strategy need some basic instruction about the nature of basic statistics (including how to use them, how not to use them, and how to visually depict them in graphs and figures)." Official research can be problematic in other ways as well. The study group Richard Nixon commissioned reported back to him that marijuana smoking was not nearly as harmful as had been previously believed, nor did it cause violent or aggressive behavior (Schafer et al. 1972). Nixon disdained the report. Instead of using the information in the report to shape public policy, he launched a war on drugs upon its release (Markham 1972).

Public policy design *produces* symbolic meaning; Schneider and Ingram's social constructivist approach shows how perceptual categories inform the policy process, and also how the policy process in turn produces its own cultural effects. "Policy designs thus structure the subsequent opportunities for participation, allocate material resources, and send messages that shape the political orientations and participation patterns of the target group as well as other members of the public. In sum, these policy designs usually reproduce the prevailing institutional culture, power relationships, and social constructions, but at times depart from this pattern and introduce change" (Ingram, Schneider, and deLeon 2007, 97).

We make the social world through actions, and we construct the beliefs upon which we act. Implicit in the social constructivist framing of reality is the presupposition of intentionality among engaged, interacting individuals. But social construction paints only part of the picture. Yes, symbolizing and categorizing create images of groups or policy targets; and, yes, images and communications inherently entail the social construction of reality through symbolic association. But the social constructivist frame leaves out of focus the symbolic material that constitutes the constructions themselves, though that is beginning to change (e.g., see Tzfadia, Levy, and Oren 2010).

B. Discourse Coalitions

Opinions, values, narratives, and feelings are all entailed in the dynamics embedded in policy discourse, although these dynamics, and the fissures and conflicts that attend the varying perspectives expressed in policy discourse, are rarely made explicit. Sabatier (1988, 131) observed that policy making emerges from social coalitions and suggested "public policies (or programs) can be conceptualized in the same manner as belief systems, i.e., as sets of value priorities and causal assumptions about how to realize them." Under the influence of their fellow conversationalists, and in the context of a changing environment, people can— eventually—change beliefs, even if their core beliefs remain intact for longer periods of time. As part of a communicative network, members of a discourse coalition can be observed behaving normatively in terms of beliefs, and some- times altruistically in ways that cast at least some doubt on the possibility of purely utilitarian, self-interested motivations presupposed by economic exchange theory (Miller 1994). Discourse—symbolically constituted meaning making— brings coherence to the policy coalition, even as it simultaneously brings coher- ence to a policy narrative. Hajer's (2005) concept of discourse coalition explicitly brings symbolic material into play in an important way. Political science cate- gories, such as interest group coalitions, can be alternatively constructed as *dis- course coalitions,* thus emphasizing the interpretive and communicative aspects of problem definition. "A discourse-coalition refers to a group of actors that, *in the context of an identifiable set of practices,* shares the usage of a particular set of story lines over a particular period of time. . . . [A] discourse-coalition is not so much connected to a particular person, but is related to practices in the context in which actors employ story lines and (re)produce and transform a particular discourse" (Hajer 2005, 302–303, emphasis in original).

To apply this concept to politics and power, Hajer (2005, 303) used the term *discourse structuration* (which occurs when a discourse begins to dominate in its policy domain) and *discourse institutionalization* (which occurs when a domi- nant discourse sediments into institutionalized practice). Hence, the story line that constitutes the discourse becomes widely accepted (a structuration process) and eventually becomes mainstream as it gains influence in informing habitual practice (institutionalization). An ensemble of story lines gets repeated among the communicators in the discourse coalition and eventually comes to inform the day-to-day practices of the policy actors involved. A fully institutionalized discourse has insinuated itself into daily practice and from this position of domi- nance asserts a particular view of reality, criticizes alternative views and stories, and enforces social positions. "If a discourse is successful—that is to say, if many people use it to conceptualize the world—it will solidify into an institution, some- times as organizational practices, sometimes as traditional ways of reasoning" (Hajer 1993, 46). Hajer analyzed the acid rain controversy by defining the prob- lem in the context of a political narrative. According to Hajer (2005, 299):

In the case of acid rain, large groups of dead trees are, of course, not a so- cial construct; the point is how one *makes sense* of dead trees. In this respect there are many possible (political) realities. One may see dead trees as the product of "natural stress" caused by drought, cold, or wind, or one may see them as victims of "pollution." Pollution can thus be seen as an ordering concept, a "way of seeing," or interpreting a given phenomenon. "Acid rain" might be constructed as an element of a narrative on industrial society and pollution. . . . [D]ead trees are no longer "an incident" but signify a "structural problem."

When these sorts of symbols and associations enter the discourse, different sets of questions are put on the agenda: Why do we tolerate dying trees? Don't we have a way of stopping this? Hence, new symbols in the language help make new causal stories. Hajer's insight here leads us deeper into a consideration of the power of language and images in public policy discourse. Category construction is a large part of the political contest when it comes to policy making. The struggle over ideas and interpretations drives the contest: How things are to be classified, what the criteria of judgment will be, and what aspirations are worthy. In public policy discourse, policy arguments are backed by narrative stories, which purport to explain how the world works. In a public policy arena, these kinds of metaphorical and narrative representations are familiar forms of political contestation and deserve to be studied. The narrative itself has the power to bring coherence to a social movement and to bind participants to it.

In addition to drawing inspiration from policy discourse research such as Hajer's, there are several other important markers in the literature that directly inform the present theoretical approach. These are briefly presented in the next and final section of this chapter.

IV. NARRATIVES EVOLVE AND FRAME MEANING

Kingdon (1984) mused about the way that symbols transform events and interpretations of events into a focus of attention. He was particularly interested in how a shorthand symbol seemed able to gather wide-reaching connotations and meanings. For him it was interesting that socially constructed symbolic meanings seemingly can be compressed into symbolic shorthand and transported efficiently among social groups, diffused throughout the relevant policy environment. Whether the symbol is "CT scan," symbolizing (to him) expensive medical technology, or "Washington METRO" as Kingdon's symbol in the late 1970s for the high cost of rail transportation (102), symbolic compression allows for high-velocity circulation of policy information and attitudes. Or as Kingdon (103) put it, "Symbols catch on and have important focusing effects because they capture in a nutshell some sort of reality that people already sense in a vaguer, more diffuse way." His most interesting consideration of symbolism concerned the evolutionary metaphors he deployed in drawing analogies between molecular communities and social communities.

A. Policy Proposals Evolve

Kingdon draws an analogy between Darwinian evolution theory and the generation of policy ideas among policy specialists; researchers; congressional staffers; people in planning, budgeting, and evaluation offices; people in academia; and interest group analysts. Generating policy ideas resembles biological evolution: "Much as molecules floated around in what biologists call the 'primeval soup' before life came into being, so ideas float around in these communities. . . . There is a long process of 'softening up': ideas are floated, bills introduced, speeches made; proposals are drafted, then amended in response to reaction and floated again. . . . The 'soup' changes not only through the appearance of wholly new elements, but even more by the recombination of previously existing elements" (Kingdon 1984, 122–123).

Capitol Hill staff members have axes to grind; lobbyists keep floating particular proposals hoping someone someday will join the cause; interest groups and researchers put forth their pet ideas. Some of the ideas gain traction, and some of them do not. Bits of information "float around the system without any hard-and-fast communication channels" (Kingdon 1984, 81). Whether policy proposals will solve actual problems is not the key factor in their generation and development. The criteria for discard or acceptance elude a priori generalization, as do the prospects for finding the origin of any particular policy idea. The search for origins or grand generalizations is less important "than the processes of mutation and recombination that occur as ideas continuously confront one another and are refined until they are ready to enter a serious decision stage" (130).

Kingdon thinks that *recombination* drives the evolution of policy ideas more so than *mutation*. "Many theorists of evolution have come to distinguish between mutation and recombination. . . . So it is with the evolution of public policy ideas. Wholly new ideas do not suddenly appear. Instead, people recombine familiar elements into a new structure or a new proposal. . . . Change turns out to be recombination more than mutation" (131). Whether the process is more like mutation or more like recombination, the evolution of public policy ideas is not merely about the power of interests. There is a field of meanings, symbolizations, ideas, and interpretations available to the policy community. They are connected by varying degrees of association, proximity, and distance. Recombination of these ideational elements accompanies policy change in any given policy context. Hence, we find in Kingdon's writing something more than windows of opportunity and policy streams. There is a nascent idea about unpredictable associations of ideas, along the lines of biological communities in a primeval stew, that only become apparent after an evolutionary period of time.

From the primeval stew, metaphors and ideographs then move along the evolutionary pathway. We are now talking about the associations of ideas not only in terms of their circulation and modes of attachment; in the narrative approach, they congeal into ideographic concepts and become an organizing force in themselves. Lakoff (2004, 17) expresses them as potentially durable mental constructions: "Concepts are not things that can be changed just by someone telling us a fact. We may be presented with facts, but for us to make sense of them, they have to fit what is already in the synapses of the brain. Otherwise facts go in and then they go right back out." This would explain why people continue to believe ideas that are demonstrably false. They have a frame, a stereotype, a narrative, an ideographic cognition, or a mental model that cannot accommodate certain dissonant facts. And it is not just "they" who transport ideas from one event to the next. Cognition itself works this way (Lakoff and Johnson 2003). Hence, the way to conduct an argument is not necessarily at the factual level, or even the experiential level, but perhaps at the ideographic level where frames and metaphors are constituted.

B. Narratives Shape Understanding

Natural scientists interpret natural phenomena; social scientists on the other hand interpret people who are themselves interpreting their worlds—a double hermeneutic (Gadamer 1996). In public policy discourse, where advocacy and political power are entailed, the prospects for objectivity seem even more remote than in other social science research. Partial views, particular points of view, and policy frameworks are in full launch when it comes time to interpret the facts of the matter. An expanding appreciation of how stories and narratives function to stabilize the decision-making environment in the face of anxious uncertainty further removes policy making from a one-dimensional technical-rational logic. Roe (1994, 2) adopted an approach that took us well beyond the seemingly irrational tendency to cling to certain frames or storylines: "The key practical insight of *Narrative Policy Analysis* is this: Stories commonly used in describing and analyzing policy issues are a force in themselves, and must be considered explicitly in assessing policy options. Further, these stories (called *policy narratives* in the book) often resist change or modification even in the presence of contradicting empirical data, because they continue to underwrite and stabilize the assumptions for decision making in the face of high uncertainty, complexity, and polarization."

Roe is not alone in pondering the way narratives congeal and stabilize. The reframing paradigm of Schön and Rein (1994), along with the narrative orientation toward policy analysis, has helped to position public policy studies on a vector that extends symbolization into the realm of meaning making and interpretation. Commitment to a narrative, consciously or unconsciously, chafes against the scientific notion that policy analysis should be neutral, objective, and open to new facts. But Kuhn's (1970) sociological study of science showed that science also operates from within narratives; he called them paradigms. Nagel (1989), in a book titled *The View from Nowhere,* mused about the human capacity for detachment that has reached the point of excess in some schools of philosophy. Even though we are often able to see a thing from multiple points of view, we all have frameworks, paradigms, standpoints, and perspectives. Scholars such as Gusfield (1981), Lakoff and Johnson (2003), and Schön and Rein (1994) have pointed out that people are pretty much compelled to deal with their political and social milieus from one framework or another if they are to maintain a sense of personhood, identity, and even competence as they face the daily flow of events. If frameworks blind us to certain other perspectives, they also enable us to see a coherent world. According to Rein and Schön (1993, 146) "framing is a way of selecting, organizing, interpreting, and making sense of a complex reality to provide guideposts for knowing, analyzing, persuading, and acting. A frame is a perspective from which an amorphous, ill-defined, problematic situation can be made sense of and acted on." Synonyms for this idea include paradigm, but also mental models, narratives, and stories. These terms capture different aspects of the way that people order their realities to interpret problematic situations and make them coherent.

Now, suppose one obstinate narrative confronts an equally obstinate and conflicting narrative. Intractable policy controversies remain unresolved. In the drug policy discourse, "just say no" abstinence competes against the "harm-reduction" narrative, a tension not necessarily relieved by the libertarian account of underground markets. Policy discourse can have more than two sides. In the environmental policy discourse, data about carbon dioxide and other greenhouse-gas emissions do not gain traction in contrarian narratives that value economic growth primarily. Recourse to objective reality, the facts, empirical evidence, or other arbiters of truth does not work to vanquish the "false" narrative while uplifting the "true" one. The other side seems always to get its facts wrong. In a narrative approach, the development of normative preferences is a matter of symbolic clustering.

In the next chapter, semiotics will bring some detail to symbolic clustering of signs and ideographs. Instead of trying to resolve differences among narratives, the narrative approach celebrates difference as an inherent feature of language.

Language has ins and outs, near and far, and similarities and differences of many kinds. In the early sections, the connotative tendencies of signs, ideographs, and narratives—problematic in some respects, liberating in others—are described and examined. Toward the end of the chapter, I will draw distinctions between readerly texts and writerly texts and draw parallels with deeply sedimented, habituated practice (readerly) and changeable practice (writerly).

3
Connotation

For the big-brained animal that speaks, the struggle over language and meaning has surpassed the more typical animal struggle over territory and food. In this chapter, meaning making depends on processes of connotation and association. Deferring to the connotative power of language, a narrative approach necessarily avoids issuing stable, authoritative definitions, as formal theory would require. Instead, the formal terms I develop in this chapter are limited to the necessary: sign, ideograph, and narrative. 1) A *sign* is the minimally meaningful symbolic element; its subparts, the signifier and the signified, become meaningful when gathered into the associative total named the *sign*. 2) *Ideographs* are collections of associated signs that connote more complex meanings, emotions, values, and imagery. Signs and ideographs are strung together by story lines to form 3) *narratives.* I begin, then, with the smallest unit of analysis, the sign and its component parts, before expanding the semiotic range of analysis to include denotation limitations, connotative expansions, and evolutionary arbitrariness.

I. SIGNIFICATION

A key concept in Saussurean semiotics is *signification* (Saussure 1983). It formally refers to the relationship between a signifier and the signified concept. Importantly, Saussure related the signifier to a *concept* but did not relate signifier to the signified *object.* Here is why this matters. If there is a pepper mill on the table, and I point to it and say "pepper mill," it seems a straightforward relationship: the signifier *pepper mill* has a direct relationship with the object, a vertical peppercorn holder with a grinder at the bottom that takes two hands to operate. But we add tremendous versatility to language usage if there doesn't have to be an actual pepper mill in our midst. *Pepper mill* is a signifier that conjures up an image of a pepper mill, even though there may be no pepper mill in the room at the moment. We do not have to carry around a physical pepper mill to have a conversation about pepper mills. If one is willing to carry around bagfuls of the objects one wishes to talk about on any given day, one need not heed this difference between concept and physical object. But I am willing to follow Saussure's lead on this one. The price for the efficiency of not having to carry around bagfuls of pepper mills and other objects is only this: we must not confuse the *concept* with the *object*. The object, even though we can pick it up and hold it, remains just out of the reach of language.

This point is worth underscoring, that words do not refer to material objects; they refer to mental pictures of those physical objects. This turns out to be a hellish problem for empiricists whose propositions rely on a one-to-one correspondence between words and reality. The relationship between indicators and facts, or variables and reality, is forever problematic. When we signify something outside of language—the "real world," a "fact," "reality itself," or "experience"—we are still only signifying concepts.

A. Language and Empiricism

The term *bear* conjures up an image of the bear, and everyone here in the room is pleased that the bear that comes into mind is a conceptual bear and not a hungry, physically present bear. And all are doubly pleased that we do not have to carry around bears in our pouches in order to have a conversation about bears. Being able to talk about a bear without having to have a bear in the room is one of the useful features of language. But this same feature of language is a bit problematic in some other ways. Think of a newspaper reporter whose job is to gather *facts* for a hard news story. The reporter wants to find the right word that directly mirrors the facts, as they happened—not the concepts. However, reporting the facts about objective reality is highly problematic if the signification system one uses can only signify concepts. The news reporter wants to be a realist, but semiotics has a storehouse full of tough problems for realists. As Edward Sapir (1929, 209–210) put it in his well-known essay "The Status of Linguistics as a Science":

> Though language is not ordinarily thought of as of essential interest to the students of social science, it powerfully conditions all our thinking about social problems and processes. Human beings do not live in the objective world alone, but are very much at the mercy of the particular language

which has become the medium of expression for their society. It is quite an illusion to imagine that one adjusts to reality essentially without the use of language and that language is merely an incidental means of solving specific problems of communication or reflection. The fact of the matter is that the "real world" is to a large extent unconsciously built upon the language habits of the group. . . . We see and hear and otherwise experience very largely as we do because the language habits of our community predispose certain choices of interpretation.

Empiricism, by contrast, would encourage the reader to interpret the message from a framework in which the signifier/signified relationship is obvious. The text has only one meaning, which is the objective and factual meaning. The empiricist insists on a single interpretation—the one that mirrors reality as intended by the makers of the message. Instead, there might be several alternative interpretations from different perspectives that would make sense.

B. Connotative Dynamics of the Sign

In semiotics, the sign gathers together both the signifier and the signified. However, according to Barthes, there is more entailed than a relation between two terms. There are three different terms. Barthes developed an analytical system in which 1) the *signifier* expresses 2) the *signified*. And 3) the *sign* meaningfully gathers both together as the associative total. As Barthes (1972, 113) put it, "For what we grasp is not at all one term after the other, but the correlation which unites them: there are, therefore, the signifier, the signified and the sign, which is the associative total of the first two terms."

Let us start with a simple example (which quickly becomes complicated). The term *rose* signifies a certain flower. Imagine a red rose with its velvety petals and thorny long stem. The *signifier* is the term *rose;* the *signified* is that pretty flower we are imagining. The associative total of this semiotic mechanism is called a *sign.* This "associative total" seems quite straightforward and denotative. But the simple denotative sign becomes nuanced as we proceed along the path toward connotation.

Now, suppose I want to signify passion, using roses. The sign *rose,* the associative total from the preceding paragraph, has now become a signifier. The thing that the signifier signifies has also shifted. Now the signified concept is passion. In this context, *roses* are now only passion-directed roses. Roses existed as roses and passion existed as passion before uniting to form this new associative total— this is the kernel of an ideograph, connoting something more expansive than a mere flower. Ah, a rose is just a rose—except when it signifies passion.

Similarly *blue sky* indicates a sky that is blue, playing its everyday role of signifier. But a *blue sky* can be made to signify in other ways. Shift context slightly;

suppose *blue sky* is a signifier of a pleasant afternoon. In the new context the term *blue sky* signifies not only the color of the sky but an emotional bearing suggestive of sunshine, clarity, or pleasantness. Signs thus come to signify something else again. And it does not end there. *Blue sky* also gets its meaning from this opposition: *red stone*. Once the "blue sky—red stone" distinction gains contextual resonance, we start thinking of oppositions such as abstract theory and concrete practice, ivory tower and real world. The connotation seems involuntary, hovering on the verge of consciousness even when not explicitly stated.

To rehearse the dynamic: 1) There is a signifier. 2) There is a signified. 3) The presence of the signified is apprehended through the signifier. Hence, meaning is generated in the associative total. Or as Barthes (1972, 113) put it: "I cannot confuse the roses as signifier and the roses as sign: the signifier is empty, the sign is full, it is a meaning." The *sign* thus reflects significance. The sign is also free to move on to other associations, to become a signifier of something else that has been connoted. This is more than simple language.

Language that functions as a mirror of reality limits itself to denotative indicators. But as a self-referential sign system, language is preoccupied with relational markers such as differences, equivalencies, and connotations. Denotations thus become connotations in infinite regress. Hence, there is no closure, no final reading or decoding, just continuous association, deconstruction, and reassembling.

The dynamic of the sign builds the ideography of a culture, as signs recombine and establish new connotations, new associations, and differences. This associative dynamic is the mechanism for making meaning. The dynamic of the sign stands in opposition to formal logic, which uses static categories in its formulations. Systems of formal logic are applied to particular contexts through indexical denotation. For example, in statistical analysis of a database, denotative links to reality are asserted by the use of indicators that are typecast into indices. Indicators, validity-enhanced by an index, mirror reality. In contrast, the dynamic of the sign does not rely on the fixity of denotation, as indicators and indices do. Instead, the sign, through its associations, emphasizes the immanence of movement, change, and meaning making, a characteristic shared with connotation.

C. Arbitrariness of the Sign

A linguistic sign is an arbitrary and conventional thing in that if we all got used to calling cats mice and dogs sheep we would still be able to communicate. The reason we think a mouse is a mouse is that we speak English. If we spoke Spanish it would be *el ratón*. Signified concepts often possess a wealth of synonymous signifiers that will lead to them. Although there are numerous signifiers that track rather closely to their signified objects—train whistles, skin rash, rustling leaves, the sound of helicopter blades—the supply of signifiers floating through culture has expanded beyond the needs of denotation alone.

Language asserts itself in a self-defining manner, oblivious to the influence of any one of us. Language seems to be self-transforming and self-regulating. It allows no appeal to a reality or authority beyond itself—it has its own reality. That a term other than *sky* might have been used to signify sky and that historical accident put *sky* in the dictionary do not take away from the power of the relationship between signifier and signified. It is doubtful that even an authoritarian dictator could decree the displacement of the signifier *sky* with some other one. Arbitrariness in origin does not diminish the power of habitual practice. The more complex the language usage, the more these cultural habits are relied upon to extend signification. We have a usefully descriptive language when the words *blue sky* denote a sky that is blue. But when *blue sky* signifies cheerfulness (as opposed to melancholy) or abstract (as opposed to concrete), we have multiple ideographic connotations being carried on the shoulders of blue sky. This gathering together of associations into cultural meanings complicates language enormously, even while empowering it.

While some terms seem overburdened with multiple meanings, others have no meaning at all. Can a signifier exist without a signified? Whenever I encounter a word whose definition I do not know, I would say yes, most certainly. What about those instances where I think I know the meaning of a word but have it wrong? In the era of the Internet, the possibility of a disconnected signifier seems easy to accept. Signifiers often replicate quickly from website to hard drive to brain without the drag effect of a signified. It is difficult to report on these free-floating signifiers because they do not convey meaning. But think of the poem by Lewis Carroll when imagining signifiers without referents:

’Twas brillig, and the slithy toves
Did gyre and gimble in the wabe:
All mimsy were the borogoves,
And the mome raths outgrabe.

But even signifiers without referents can develop meaning. Having watched the movie *Alice in Wonderland,* I now know what a *frumious Bandersnatch* looks like. The signifier has linked up with a signified (the beast in the movie) to develop a meaningful sign. The term now has a conceptual image attached to it, and so graduates from signifier to sign. As signifiers develop meaning and associations, they become more complex, gathering in affective components. They also develop recognition.

An analogy to this process is the random mutation and natural selection of evolutionary biology. Environmental selection accounts for why there is clover on the hill as opposed to grass. An arbitrary weather variation put clover seeds in the air during the wet season under an unusual northeasterly wind several years ago, which nobody noticed at the time. And now the clover on the hill certainly seems to belong there. The clover seeds are like arbitrary signs that go blowing through the Internet and eventually establish themselves, first in e-mail in-boxes and Facebook pages and then in the brains of the computer user, through repetition and human usage. Yet, their foundational reason for being may be as capricious as the wind. This is the arbitrariness of the sign.

Saussure's "arbitrariness of the sign" generated doubt about the surety with which we affix a signifier to the signified. Suppose that we wanted to signify the concept *empty conversation*. The term for the signifier could be "yadda yadda yadda" or it could be "blah blah blah" or it could be "empty conversation." Accidents of cultural context sometimes favor one or the other, but attempting to discover a universal principle for how language affixes signifiers to concepts is unlikely to bring results. Many neologisms disappear before they achieve habitual usage. Saussure's advice would be to accept this context-specific building of meaning as arbitrary. Lies, errors, misunderstandings, misspellings, mispronunciations, and eccentric interpretations can all serve to connect/disconnect the signifier to/from the signified concept. Software programs have been developed to randomly produce grammatically correct paragraphs that are nonetheless devoid of conceptual intelligence. It is as if signifiers play with one another freely, without the discipline of being attached to a signified. Random-text generators on the Internet seem to be making this very point.

Barthes (1977b, 39) noted the anxious human need to *fix* a chain of signifiers that seem to be floating without foundation. *Anchorage* refers to the notion that linguistic elements are able to anchor (constrain) the reading of an image to a preferred one. While anchorage would reduce anxiety, help the communicators gain closure on meaning, and tether the signs to a stable interpretation, such stability is made only of cultural habit and history. Sometimes signs behave as if well anchored on permanent mooring at the bottom of the harbor, but other times the anchor drags. In semiotics, the meaning of signs is not usually volatile, but the meaning is, nonetheless, changeable. When we talk about drug consumer and habitué and then addict, are we still talking about the same person? Semiotics always leaves room for another question.

The wondrous ability of words to mingle among themselves and generate new meanings has captivated many a wordsmith. Word play—poetry, for example—does not sever a word from its meaning so much as multiply the possible array of available meanings. The signifier can become the signified when deployed in a different context—metaphors do this kind of work. Meaning may be ambiguous in these word performances, but the elasticity of signification is what allows images, myths, ideologies, and ideographs to build meanings and change them.

D. Difference and Association

Saussure (1983) also got us thinking of language in terms of differences. For example, slight differences in sound—*mad* as opposed to *bad*—give a spoken word a different meaning. This ascription of different meanings to different sounds may have been arbitrary at one point in time, but now meanings of different sounds are firmly entrenched in the culture and would be difficult if not impossible for any one person to alter.

The notion of difference relies on Saussure's thinking of the *signified* as a concept rather than the more commonsense notion that the signified is the object itself. This move, this way of thinking about signifiers as concepts rather than objects in themselves, allows signs to gain meaning from one another. Saussure argued that concepts are defined not in terms of their content (e.g., the blueness of blue or the roundness of a circle) but in contrast to coexisting signs of the same sign system. A sign that is part of a meaning system, rather than a mirror of reality, can perform this feat of meaning generation. Hence, blue is *not red; not green; not yellow*, etc. Circle is *not square; not triangle; not parallelogram*. Highway is *not lane, not street, not road*, and so on. These terms function in language systems to generate meaning when contrasted with opposing or different terms. The real world is not a fantasy world. Fact is not fiction. Difference is but one of the ways signs associate with one another.

Barthes (1977a, 71) identified affinity of sound (violets are *blue*, and I love *you*) and affinity of meaning (a *chain of command* is like a *hierarchy*) as forms of association. Further examples of association include: *bread* can be used to *nourish; clothing* can be used as *protection from elements* or as *fashion*. On the roadways, *red* means *stop* while *green* means *go*. In an oppositional way, *fast* is associated with *slow* and *near* is associated with *far*. In public policy discourse, new associations are invented, fabricated, asserted, repeated, and otherwise interjected into narratives on a regular basis. Attaching a new signified to an already existing signifier is how one makes analogies. Types of analogies—metaphor, metonymy, trope, synecdoche, synonym, and so on—build up the richness of symbolic association over time to the point that the associations eventually seem literal. It is easy to forget that at some historical point it was not literally self-evident that rivers have mouths, or that bottles have necks, or that traffic accidents during rush hour cause bottlenecks. (See Davidson 2001, 252.) What was once metaphorical and connotative can, with regular usage, become literal and seemingly denotative. Perhaps a new idea, to gain currency, must somehow associate itself—as oppositional or affirmative—with that same culture's already-existing field of ideographs that are active or latent in the cultural archives, the culture's stock of imprints.

Connotations can be sufficiently obscure that users of the language are themselves not conscious of them, as an example from an insurance investigator illustrates.

E. Mutant Metaphors

As an insurance investigator in the 1920s, Benjamin Lee Whorf realized that physical context alone was not sufficient explanation in accounting for fire hazards. In particular, language played a role in obfuscating the danger of an empty gasoline drum.

> Thus, around a storage of what are called "gasoline drums," behavior will tend to a certain type, that is, great care will be exercised; while around a storage of what are called "empty gasoline drums," it will tend to be different—careless, with little repression of smoking or of tossing cigarette stubs about. Yet the "empty" drums are perhaps the more dangerous, since they contain explosive vapor. Physically, the situation is hazardous, but the linguistic analysis according to regular analogy must employ the word *empty*, which inevitably suggests a lack of hazard. The word *empty* is used in two linguistic patterns: (1) as a virtual synonym for "null and void, negative, inert," (2) applied in analysis of physical situations without regard to, e.g., vapor, liquid vestiges, or stray rubbish, in the container. (Whorf 1997, 135)

This association of the word *empty* with lack of hazard provided Whorf, on his way to becoming a noted semiotician, an insight into the way that meanings can serve as limiters as much as enablers of understanding. The term *empty* possessed sedimented ideographic meaning that failed to take into account the idea that a container holding little more than vapor could be even more flammable than a container full of gasoline.

In linguistics there are moments when a spelling changes, when *through* becomes *thru,* or when *dialogue* becomes *dialog.* It may happen in some subculture of the population, perhaps road-sign makers or efficient newspaper editors. When a signifier, *twitter* for example, emerges in the lexicon to refer to a system of message sending and receiving and then enters the dictionary under this new definition, we have another moment of language change. Twitter is no longer just about chirping or walking like a sand bird. The term has combined with technology to signify a communications medium. Reading or listening to Robert

Burns's "On turning up her nest with the plough" signals so many of these mutations that it seems like the poem could have been written in a language other than English. Americans have gone so far as to spell *plough plow*. Another associative mutation takes place when a signifier's meaning shifts. For example *surfing*, once a water sport, morphed into sidewalk surfing, then channel surfing, and then surfing the web, subsequently displaced by Googling. Signifiers are borrowed from a different signified concept quite frequently. Alteration of signs takes place through the shifting of association. The term *liberal* was used in the Enlightenment to challenge the divine right of kings to rule the land. In the United States that meaning gave way over the years to connote regulation of business, economic fairness, and social welfare programs. The term then morphed into a conservative political complaint (in the American lexicon) intended to ascribe permissiveness, wishy-washy tolerance, and excess indulgence to certain viewpoints. In other parts of the world, liberal and neoliberal refer to assertive styles of capitalism. Hence, meaning change is culture specific if not situation specific.

II. DENOTATION/CONNOTATION

The notion that a sign mirrors reality is a presupposition that Vienna Circle logical positivists found compelling (Fox and Miller 1997). Logical positivism had as one of its main goals the elimination of metaphysics from science. The word *metaphysics* was used as a pejorative catchall term under which theology, ethics, myths, psychoanalysis, phrenology, alchemy, intuition, and astrology could be dismissed. Words that did not mirror reality were turned away as poetry. To count as science, statements must be definable in terms of observables. This strict regimen of fundamentalist science lasted only so long. Logical positivists eventually admitted that many scientifically useful terms were not verifiable as observable fact. The key criterion of denotative verifiability was compromised when it became undeniable that in scientific practice terms are frequently defined relative to one another and often without reference to observable facts. Denotative words could not themselves mirror reality.

Connotative words do not follow the austere and strict discipline that denotation demands. Connotation suggests multiple concepts, images, associations, and interpretations. Semiotics has developed a useful framework for grasping the reality directness of signifiers. Following Chandler (2002) the following three semiotic modes vary from directly denotative to connotative:

1. Index/indexical: The signifier is directly connected to the signified. Examples include smoke, thunder, paw prints, skin rash, pulse rate, weather-

cock, a knock on the door, a telephone ringing, a barking dog, a photo-graph, or someone's signature.

2. Icon/iconic: The signifiers *resemble* something, for example, a portrait, a cartoon caricature of a politician, onomatopoeia (such as quack, woof, or meow), or realistic sounds like bang, crash, zoom, or whoosh.

3. Symbol/symbolic: These are purely conventional signifiers in that their meaning is socially constructed. The relationships between signifier and sign must be learned through some type of education, acculturation, or socialization.

The reality status of the sign is a troublesome matter for those who do not heed Saussure's lesson that, when not indexical, the signifier points to a concept and not an object. Empiricism's function for language is to mirror reality, so that the link between the words and whatever object is being depicted is as un-mediated as possible, as identical as possible. Otherwise, there is distortion of reality. However, the inherent limitations of language prohibit this aspiration from ever being completely realized. In language usage, there is no reunion with "reality itself." The narrative approach does not deny the existence of an objec-tive world outside of any individual or culturally ethnographic interpretation of it, but there is not a world we can talk about that exists outside a culture and its language. There is no preordained content stored within the terms *reality, fact,* or *experience*. Interpretation of reality or text entails a culture-bound perspec-tive that does not necessarily announce itself as ethnocentric. All perspectives are partial, so the presupposition that the terms used are neutral, natural, and innocent is always problematic. For example, as deployed in the dominant drug policy narrative, *drug addict* wants to claim factual denotation. Instead, deno-tation nearly always turns out to be another instance of connotation, once its dubious naturalization is exposed and its literalness is revealed as illusory. *Drug addict* is ideographically connotative, gathering in values, emotional attitudes, normative judgments, psychological and biological typologies, imagined visual settings, perhaps a recalled stench or an empathic memory, and so on.

The polysemic imagery of symbolic connotation contrasts sharply with the specificity of indexical and iconic denotation, with large implications for the functioning of language in policy discourse. Words are suggestive and seem un-willing to stand still and play the role of denotative, empirical indicator. Perhaps this is why botanists use Latin names for plants, to preserve the denotative power of the descriptors by shielding them as much as possible from connotative cor-rosion. "Connotative phenomena have not yet been systematically studied. . . . Yet the future probably belongs to a linguistics of connotation, for society con-tinually develops, from the first system which human language supplies to it, second-order significant systems, and this elaboration, now proclaimed and now disguised, is very close to a real historical anthropology" (Barthes 1977a, 90).

The differences between denotation and connotation help in understanding some the difficulties facing the policy analyst who must mediate between knowledge and politics. The overarching question of meaning vexes both estates, especially when meaning shifts.

III. THE IDEOGRAPH AS CONNOTATIVE CLUSTER

An ideograph is a type of symbolic material that might inform a policy narrative, though it has not necessarily been appropriated into any particular policy narrative. Saussure (1983, 13) described the term *stock of imprints* as a social product that generates a social bond through language. This is close to the meaning of ideographs, which are also embedded in history and culture. They play a regulatory role and function in political communication to warrant action by referencing a culturally familiar image or a socially acceptable symbolic rationale.

Drug addict is an example of an ideograph that conjures up symbolic imagery. Both a criminal narrative and the very different disease narrative make use of the drug addict ideograph. In the criminal narrative, the drug addict deserves punishment, and in the disease narrative the drug addict needs health care. Ideograph is thus a middle-ground indicator of symbolization, not so fixed and determined that it cannot be appropriated by competing narratives but sufficiently stable as a constellation of meaning to serve as a nodal point in a story line. An ideograph functions at a level of symbolization that is more connotative than a word or a simple sign but, at the same time, not as thematically coherent as narrative would be.

By focusing on ideographs and the story lines that make use of them, it quickly becomes apparent that one is not merely arguing with "these same people" over some contentious matter; rather, one narrative is in contest with another narrative. By displacing the individual or some aggregations of individuals (group, population) as unit of analysis, symbolic units such as signs, ideographs, and narratives reorient attention to the struggle over meaning capture and the strategic arranging of ideographic images, values, arguments, and so on. Ordinarily there is nothing constitutive of any of the competing narratives that would not already be circulating in the culture.

Ideography is concerned with semantic associations, with similarities and differences in symbolic meanings. The term *addiction* signifies in various ways; someone may be addicted to chocolate or some television show or love or gambling. *Drug*, too, connotes different images in different settings; when invoked in *drug store* it seems like part of an everyday errand. However, when drug and addict are invoked together, these two signs signal *drug addiction,* and the connotation combines parts of both signs to form an ideograph. While not the complete story, ideographs pull together multiple signs and references—the materials that can be readily appropriated into cultural narratives. An ideograph encapsulates a sufficient mass of symbolic meaning that can be accessed by only some of the different narratives, ideologies, and myths circulating in society. *Childhood obesity* is used in a preventive health care narrative but probably would not work in many others. An ideograph rarely tells a story on its own, even though some ideographs may be single purpose in their usage (for example, *partial birth abortion*). Ideographs typically need a story line to attain closure and completeness. Some ideographs are deployed in a wide range of narratives and policy stories: *fairness, efficiency, loyalty, freedom, objective facts, security, prosperity,* and *welfare* are some common ones in the public policy literature. Ideographs are often invoked to influence policy deliberation, as when DDT was causally linked to dead robins, or when acid rain was linked to dead trees. Ideographs contribute to the political altering of ideas and social practices. As units of analysis, ideographs are symbolic framing constructs, abstractions that are, nonetheless, capable of warranting peoples' sense of what is and what is not reality; what is and is not appropriate action.

A. Narrative

Gathering together story lines that connect multiple ideographs, narrative brings its coherence to policy discourse. Narrative is the most complex framing device to be considered in this book. Public policy can change things when entrenched narratives are changed. Ideography readily accommodates such discursive shifts. An ideograph registers pictures, images, symbols, impressions, and meaning systems that are widely shared in the culture yet open to wide-ranging use and abuse and open to redescription as part of a different narrative. For example, *medical marijuana* connotes vastly different imagery than the *reefer madness* of the 1930s.

Narratives can become powerful carriers of images and ideographs and are also necessarily culture specific. Americans often tell their life stories in terms of advancement from humble origins—generalized from the rags-to-riches storyline template. Redemption stories—I was once down and out but now I'm back on my feet and doing well—abound in the culture. Twelve-step programs are but one narrative of the genre. Similarly, emancipation stories tell of a struggle to get out of a bad situation at home, in an institution, or from a network of controlling substances and acquaintances. These stories serve as narrative vehicles on which ideographic images and associations can take a joy ride.

As symbolizations move from sign to ideograph to narrative, their connotative complexity increases. Barthes regarded myth as the ultimate narrative, the grand organizing narrative of a culture. "However paradoxical it may seem, *myth hides nothing:* its function is to distort, not make disappear" (Barthes 1972, 121). For Barthes, signification is the myth itself. If I read Barthes aright, making something significant is itself a form of distortion. To make significant, one must bring to the foreground something, leaving the rest of the things in the background. Moreover, myth crowds out other myths, making them fade into the background. "The nature of the mythical signification can in fact be well conveyed by one particular simile: it is neither more nor less arbitrary than an ideograph. Myth is a pure ideographic system, where the forms are still motivated by the concept which they represent while not yet, by a long way, covering the sum of its possibilities for representation" (127).

Myth and grand narrative gather in ideographic images with story lines that are imbued with emotions, character, values, meanings, and logics. Similarly, but from a knowledge perspective, an episteme for Foucault (1970) is a sufficiently stable era in the pattern of thought that there is one regime of truth that defines the conditions of knowledge. There is a singular cultural code that governs language, perception, and values. The danger of myth (or grand narrative or episteme) is to take as universal that which is ethnocentric; narratives are necessarily perspectival. In *Archaeology of Knowledge,* Foucault (1982) instead uses the term *discursive formation.* Discursive formation, like episteme, signifies a set of symbols that authorize knowledge, but only in a context and with more malleability and less universalizing aspirations than the term *episteme* implies. That multiple narratives, contradictory to one another but coherent within their own meaning perspectives, can coexist in drug policy discourse is evidence of the perspectivism that necessarily accompanies narrative analysis.

Myth, too, is perspectival, even though Barthes (1972, 142) characterizes myth as narrative that has become so thoroughly embedded in culture that it has lost all controversy, all politics, all doubt. Some stories, concepts, and meanings are so sufficiently habituated that they are taken as given, as the foundational and noncontroversial meanings to which new meaning-making activities must defer.

B. Readerly/Writerly

Barthes (1975, 4) distinguished between a readerly text and a writerly text, likening a readerly text to a sort of classic text that maintains a "pitiless divorce" between the producer of the text and its user: "This reader is thereby plunged into a kind of idleness—he is intransitive; he is, in short, *serious:* instead of functioning himself, instead of gaining access to the magic of the signifier, to the pleasure of writing, he is left with no more than the poor freedom either to accept or reject the text: reading is no more than a *referendum.*" Elaborating on

Barthes's insight, Hawkes (1977) took this to mean that *readerly texts* (e.g., classics or Barthes's grand myth) are fixed and static. They read themselves and perpetuate an established view of reality and values, which are frozen in time. They presuppose an unquestioned and solidly anchored relationship between signifier and signified.

Readerly texts might be books considered sacred by literal-minded religious fundamentalists. If challenging a certain text is considered to be an act of blasphemy, one can be fairly certain that the challenged narrative is interpreted to be a readerly text. An ideographic democracy, on the other hand, would consist of symbolic associations that are not fixed permanently but are open to reinterpretation and choice. Metaphors would be allowed to mutate. Ideographic democracy implies that new associations are allowed, new attempts at meaning making are permitted, and blasphemies and heresies are treated as competing views rather than punishable offenses against the reigning episteme.

Properties of a readerly text versus a writerly text do not inhere to the texts themselves, but to the interpretation one imposes on the text. The U.S. Constitution is both readerly (in demanding that it be taken as authoritative for everyone in its domain) and writerly (it allows itself to be amended, and it has been). However, some texts are sufficiently ubiquitous in a culture as to seem preinterpreted—and this idea of a preinterpreted text gets to the essence of the *readerly text*. Sex categories such as male and female have been readerly texts for years and only recently have been called into question—which is to say, only recently have become writerly texts for a subset of the culture. Categories of sexual identity such as transgender provide a case in point; identity is no longer cisgendered necessarily (that is, there is not necessarily a match between one's body gender and identity). One can identify as transgendered or one of many other third-gender or nongender categories. To say that the use of gender categories other than male or female is heretical or blasphemous is to speak from the perspective of a narrative that aspires to be a readerly text. Like the presupposition that body and gender match, descriptions of *human nature* bring with them a plethora of presuppositions. For example, the proposition that humans are utility-maximizing, gain-seeking, self-interested individuals remains a readerly presupposition in much economic thought.

Secular literature tends toward allowably open interpretation; hence, most narratives are writerly texts. *Writerly texts* involve us in the dangerous and exhilarating activity of creating our world *now,* together with the author, as we go along. In writerly texts, there are no presuppositions about an automatic linkage between signifier and signified. These texts are open to the play of meanings. Readerly texts march; writerly texts dance (Hawkes 1977). Readerly texts want order; writerly texts have climactic moments when order breaks down, as during fissures, impasses, and discontinuity. Writerly texts have dynamism and velocity whereas readerly texts are familiar yet sluggish. Writerly texts thus challenge the order and the safe anchorage that are essential to foundationalisms. Writerly texts show there is no permanently clear mirror of reality, only a roomful of distorting mirrors. Much of what we see is inscribed on the lens itself—scratches, rose coloring, fingerprints, religious staining, and so on. Worse, we may well be looking *at* the lens, not *through* it. Texts function as a *message,* not a *medium* through which reality is conveyed. The distorted mirrors, stained glass windows, and inscribed lenses are cultural products.

On the other hand, maintenance and reinforcement of social order depends on the readerly texts, or something like them, to generate shared views and common values. Particular visions of reality are institutionalized in these grand narratives. Hence, the classic texts and their readerly interpretations presented and re-presented in the educational system serve as normalizing rehearsals for the socialization process. Chandler (2002, 205) takes the point further, noting that even the seemingly natural "experience" is prefigured by the conceptual equipment we take into the moment we call experience: "Texts are instrumental not only in the construction of other texts but in the construction of experiences. Much of what we 'know' about the world is derived from what we have read in books, newspapers and magazines, from what we have seen in the cinema and on television and from what we have heard on the radio." Life is lived through the symbolizations we encounter as much as through "reality" or "experience." A further point needs to be made here. Convention is not innocent. The classic conventional text, politically bolstered by cultural habits and sedimented habits, fends off the upstart competition.

Deeply embedded, institutionalized conventions may seem out of reach of politics and therefore not debatable. But when readerly texts are taken to be writerly texts, we can make and remake the institutionalized conventions of meaning as we please, to the extent that we can. If writerly texts over time can become readerly texts, and readerly texts can revert back to writerly texts, does anything have permanent meaning? The sound of the telephone ringing will always mean that someone is trying to call—until it no longer means that, for example, when everyone has a cell phone and the association no longer applies. Our subjectivity is continually being created and re-created by the nonconventions (fashions, fads, free-floating signifiers) as well as the conventions (traditions and established practices) that inscribe themselves onto our personages. While technologies such as the printing press, radio, television, telephones, and the Internet work wonders to increase the velocity of signifiers in circulation, there are forces at work to slow this process down as well. Among these forces is the heavy weight of cultural habit conveyed by readerly texts—metaphors for institutionalized social practices. Cultural habit is its own form of power even though institutionalized social practice amounts to little more than a *habitual comportment* to behave *this* way, which is how we always behave, instead of *that* way. Comportments are manners of conduct shaped by one's orientation to the social context. Acceptable ways of doing things have regularized themselves into habit.

If regularized habit describes a practice, political contestation is about changing that practice—or not. Political contestation attempts to make contingent that which has been taken as second nature, that which has been presupposed and assumed to be true, natural, and indisputable. It is possible to repoliticize these taken-for-granted practices; here the analogy would be the writerly text. Political contestation unfolds through political processes that challenge some practices or their justifications or the beliefs that undergird them. The challenge may not prevail; defense of these same practices, justifications, and beliefs may enable their further sedimentation into cultural habitus. Hence, the aim of politics is to challenge status quo practices and institutions or, from the status quo perspective, to fend off potentially challenging narratives. Practices can again be called into question, thus enabling the possibility of new meanings, practices, and identities. The distinction between readerly texts and writerly texts helps to illuminate the tension between status quo ways and new possibilities.

In this section ideographs were presented as connotative and holistic symbolic units of analysis. Their semiotic value is not their denotative precision but their symbolic integration of meaning into recognizable symbolizations. Ideographs are open to reinterpretation. New associations (including negative associations such as differences) are asserted; new attempts at meaning making are permitted. Signs and ideographs evolve through associations with other signs and ideographs and, over time, are linked by story lines into narrative. The narrative may further stabilize into something more like a readerly text. The next section summarizes the chapter by focusing on the ways meaning may change.

IV. CHANGING MEANING

Language can be changed using irony, metaphor, allegory, or any other trope that makes meaning move. The moment of language change (mutation, recombination) could be any of these:

• Signifier/sign: For example, the signifier *marijuana* displaces the signifier *hemp,* emphasizing not only a connection to Mexican culture but also the mood-altering feature of cannabis rather than its rope-making attributes.

- Sign/sign association: The sign marijuana is associated in the 1930s with the signs murder and menace.
- Sign/sign difference: Resource conservation differs from environmental preservation in environmental policy discourse.
- Sign/ideograph: "Three strikes and you're out" gathers in more than a baseball rule.
- Ideograph/story line: Drugs addicts need health care.
- Story line/narrative: Drug policy should be guided by the harm-reduction principle.

This list of bullet points is certainly not an exhaustive listing of the kinds of associations that can form in the evolution of symbolic meaning. Narratives can combine with other narratives, for example; or a sign can be appropriated into a narrative without first joining the connotative cluster of an ideograph. Meanings seem to evolve over time; ideographs are interpreted differently in different narratives; connotations that seem like second nature—that roses signify passion—are typically culture specific. While patterns in the changes of meaning seem not to be regular enough for predictions, there could be a time dimension or a historical context that undergirds meaning. Similarly, diachronic change in the meaning of words over time has both history and context working in its favor. In public policy discourse, diachronic evolution of meaning occurs as signs become more connotative, gathering multiple associations to become ideographs deployed in policy narratives.

The competition among signs and ideographs and narratives does not imply that the best narrative wins; only that the winning narrative has won for the time being, which could be for years or even centuries. The symbolic material generated through the evolutionary dynamics of replication/imitation (of signs, ideographs, story lines, and narratives) develops its associations in fits and starts. The narrative approach would not affirm "survival of the fittest" notions of progress in discursive evolution. Nor would a narrative approach convey some kind of progress toward ever more meaningful meaning—surely there are meaning-destroying influences of, say, high-velocity Internet information that extinguish previous meanings. Yet, an understandable picture of historical development of practice can be painted by focusing on the associations and recombinations of ideas and metaphors as they evolve.

An organizational analogy to this evolutionary idea is Giddens's (1984) structuration theory, in which institutions are understood not as reified abstractions but rather as norms and ways of doing things that are reiterated through daily practice. Institutionalized habitual practices bring order to everyday life. We become predictable to one another, thus enabling cooperative effort. Diachronic, historically built-up narratives provide a common understanding that warrants conduct. Narratives are more than interesting reading; they help us distinguish between appropriate and inappropriate behavior. Regularized (institutionalized) social practices are the very material of social order and cultural stability. This outlook is commonly appreciated in sociology and is particularly germane to public policy and administration. Public policy discourse reveals the knowledge, rationales, and operations that justify, explain, and legitimate the prevailing regime of social practices. At the same time, proposals to change those same established practices are also justified and legitimated through policy discourse.

Public policy discourse weaves the raw materials of culture—signifiers and ideographs—into coherent narratives, hence, promoting social order and meaningful change, while legitimizing and establishing social practices (social practices being a major topic of the next two chapters). Public policy discourse is one way of refining the raw material, though the coherence generated in the refinement process may not be rational coherence. Much of that refinement occurs through selection, exclusion, recombination, and association of symbolic material such as signs, ideographs, and narratives. Public policy making has a distinctive, though not entirely unique, role in legitimizing social practices once a particular narrative interpretation is formally endorsed through social and political protocols.

Meaning is accomplished for a signifier through association. A signifier connects with a signified concept; further association with some other sign may generate more meaning. Signs become signifiers to connote some additional meaning, as when rose comes to signify passion. From this material an ideograph can grow. For example, the term *opiate* connects with the concept *narcotics* and then with the sign *addict* to generate a powerful image: *narcotics addict.* Story lines, narratives, and policy prescriptions emerge from important moments such as these. *Narcotics addicts are dangerous to the community and should be imprisoned.*

Communications that recombine symbolic material by weaving associations and connoting different interpretations require a capacity to accommodate complex symbolic meaning systems. Longer story lines generate the possibility of still-further development of narratives. Full-blown narratives rely on signs and ideographs made coherent through story lines. Decades later, with assistance from signs, ideographs, and narratives, the signifier has replicated onto perhaps hundreds or millions of brains. Now everybody, it seems, calls the stuff marijuana rather than hemp or cannabis. Its connotative associations have expanded into ideographs via cooperation and association (including oppositional association) with other signs, thus becoming part of a narrative or many narratives. The language's meaning changes ever so slightly when a new sign is brought into the picture. *Medical marijuana,* for example, has changed the drug's meaning. Opportunities for change in culture and its social practices emerge because the new ideographic arrangement warrants different modes of appropriate conduct.

How policy information is served can affect how it is perceived, as different cultures and subgroups have different stylistic tastes. A particular policy priority would not find its moment amidst all the clutter unless and until a policy image—the sign, ideograph, or narrative—competed successfully against status quo imagery by first surviving long enough to gain traction and then by finding the right moment to expand against the powerful institutional forces that support the status quo arrangements and resist or co-opt new information and new signs. The original arbitrariness of signifiers does not prevent them from evolving into meaningful symbolizations. They cohere into cultural ideographs or images that bundle together a complex of signs into intelligible knowledge, values, emotions, and meanings. This ideography does not add up to a mirror of reality but rather gains pride of place in the cultural archives, which can be accessed by those seeking to interpret, persuade, or imagine new meaning (or reinforce the prevailing interpretation). Ideography is stored in the cultural archives, ready to be checked out and borrowed at will and used again and changed again in the making of meaning.

I have drawn analogies between readerly texts and habitual practice, and writerly texts and political contestation, but have not yet transformed symbolic material into policy performance, the task of the next two chapters. Chapter 4 reasserts the political into public administration, and chapter 5 will bring narrative performance into the theory.

4
The Politics of
Changing Practices

In this chapter, I first portray the realm of practice, exemplified by public administration, as thoroughly imbued with the potential for political challenge. Public administration's façade of neutrality recalls the strategy of the readerly text, but in the daily practices of public administration the writerly text is in evidence, particularly at moments of impasse. The tension generated in the contest between changing practices and maintaining a stable order makes public administration a preeminent site for politics. Then I propose that the dynamic that melds narrative and practice is a symbiotic relationship.

I. POLITICS IN PUBLIC ADMINISTRATION

Let's begin with a striking disconnect that appears in the public administration literature: the dramatic politics of the U.S. Forest Service's political beginnings, reported in appendix 2, is not part of the story in Herbert Kaufman's public administration classic, *The Forest Ranger*. Had the Forest Service been drained of its politics by 1960, when it was appreciated as a well-run government agency but not remembered as the living legacy of the once-emergent conservation narrative? Kaufman (1960, xxvii) states in the preface that his book "does not deal with the processes in which such policy is formed, or with the desirability or defects of prevailing policy, or with measures that might improve policy or the methods of policy formulation. In a general way, current policy is taken as a 'given.'" He then proceeds to drive the point home. He notes that his book is not about the political life of the U.S. Forest Service; not about its institutional environment and relations with other agencies; not about cooperation with state-level governmental agencies; not about institutional protection or expansion of jurisdiction or power; not about strategic compromises; and not about bureaucratic politics. "All that is relevant here is that the men in the field are apparently doing what the top officers want done in the field; the study aims at explaining how the wishes of the latter are transformed into the actions of the former" (xxix).

We are all products of our times, and, of course, Kaufman was no exception. His commitment to study the machinations inside an organization resonated with the intellectual mood of 1960s behaviorism. In the isolated closed-system organization of the time, management and control displaced history and political environment. For example, Kaufman framed the Forest Service's strategic compromises and cooperation with state-level agencies as a simple matter of fact rather than an unstable arrangement that came on the heels of political struggle. The single-minded focus on managerial control displaces history and politics, offering instead an instrumental focus on operations, perceived as ahistorical. His declarative style of enunciating factuality downplays the political commotion that has played out in the scope and direction of the U.S. Forest Service's mission: "Management of timber and control of fire are the chief activities, but recreation and wildlife protection have arisen sharply in importance in recent years" (9). The political and social forces that gave rise to that change in mission—such as the evolving preservation narrative—are set off to the margins in Kaufman's presentation, as if genesis amnesia has afflicted the U.S. Forest Service. There is no notice taken of either the corruption that the U.S. Forest Service confronted in its early years or the high value placed on conservation that inspired the early forest rangers.

As the first head of the U.S. Forest Service from 1905 to 1910, Gifford Pinchot drew the line on corruption. He confronted Secretary of the Interior Richard Ballinger for conflict of interest because Ballinger represented Clarence Cunningham as a private attorney, but as a public official (at the General Land Office before it was transferred from Interior to Agriculture) he helped move Cunningham's dubious coal claims through the system. The Cunningham/Ballinger scheme saw Ballinger-as-attorney representing Cunningham in the courts after Ballinger-as-public-official steered Cunningham's land claims through the Department of Interior. President Taft eventually exonerated Ballinger but in doing so alienated the former president Roosevelt and exposed a fissure in the Republican Party. Ballinger's case was unique in its public controversy, but the appropriation of public resources was not unusual. Even so, there were rare prosecutions of timber thieves or con artists making phony land claims, though, notably, Sen. John H. Mitchell of Oregon was indicted and convicted of having received bribes for expediting the land claims of clients before the U.S. Land Commissioner (Biographical Directory of the United States Congress, undated). I raise the issue of corruption to underscore the point that contemporary norms and practices in the U.S. Forest Service have a historical backdrop that gives them context. The norms were shaped by interactions and relationships that generated politics and, eventually, a particular regime of practices favored by management. But with chapters titled "Detecting and Discouraging Deviation," "Procedural Devices for Performing Decisions," and "Developing the Will and Capacity to Conform," Kaufman framed Forest Service practices as a managerial triumph sans politics, history, or cultural context.

Goodsell's (2011) report on meanings and belief systems at six public administration agencies in the United States presents a stark contrast to Kaufman's preoccupation with managerial control. Goodsell is attentive to belief systems within public agencies. At the U.S. National Park Service, the U.S. National Weather Service, the U.S. Centers for Disease Control and Prevention, the Mecklenburg (NC) Department of Social Services, the Virginia State Police, and the U.S. Peace Corps, there were strong feelings about attention to history, pride in expertise, and the need to adapt to ever-changing circumstances (from the rise of HIV to Hurricane Katrina) and political realities. There was less inward focusing on neutral managerial processes, but rather constant interrogation of internal practices juxtaposed against broader socio-cultural and natural events. Indeed, at the National Park Service—which came into being amidst the same conservation-preservation policy discourse that brought into being the U.S. Forest Service discussed in appendix 2—managerial technique itself was often a problematic political issue. "Some said morale has dropped in recent years because top management became oriented toward largely irrelevant performance measures and ignored the concerns of subordinates" (Goodsell 2011, 43). Despite complaints about these and other management issues, "throughout the discussion a fundamental faith in the importance of the mission was expressed" (44), and current park rangers sometimes recounted memories of visiting a park as a child. Values such as "protecting the country's natural resources, as well as keeping America beautiful" (45) were defended. Some rangers missed the olden days before large corporations took over what were once family-run concessions, leading to commercial interests sometimes superseding mission values. While Kaufman's Forest Service did not have much of a political life, Goodsell's Park Service did. In the first decade of the twenty-first century, the Park Service was ordered not to remove religious plaques; it was ordered to stock the Grand Canyon bookstore with a book that provided a creationist rather than geological explanation of the canyon. When proposals were floated to relax rules on cell phone towers, grazing, mining, and environmental protection, the Coalition of National Park Service Retirees mobilized political action to head off the changes. There were other political controversies during that time period about how many snowmobiles per day would be allowed in Yellowstone National Park, the opening of all national parks and refuges to guns (passed into law in February 2010), the budget of the National Park Service, and privatization of services (Goodsell 2011). Within the agency, policy discourse and contestation of current and imagined practice was alive and well, just as Friedrich (1940) would have expected. Regarding Frank J. Goodnow's distinction between the expression of the will of the state and the execution of that will, Friedrich (1940, 116) wrote: "But while the distinction has a great deal of value as a relative matter of emphasis, it cannot any longer be accepted in this absolute form. Admittedly, this misleading distinction has become a fetish, a stereotype in the minds of theorists and practitioners alike." To emphasize the point, Friedrich (1940, 117) asked a rhetorical question:

> Will anyone understand better the complex processes involved in the articulation of this important public policy if we talk about the expression and the execution of the state will? The concrete patterns of public policy formation and execution reveal that politics and administration are not two mutually exclusive boxes, or absolute distinctions, but that they are two closely linked aspects of the same process. Public policy, to put it flatly, is a continuous process, the formation of which is inseparable from its execution. Public policy is being formed as it is being executed, and it is likewise being executed as it is being formed.

In practice, public administration and politics are tightly intertwined, and it would be wrong to think of administration as politically neutral or policy free. In discourse theory, politics is inherent in the contestable vocabularies used in the organization, the practices that have been adopted that might one day be changed, the techniques utilized, and the narratives that dominate or are challenged. Operations inside the organization are inherently political and, moreover, the external politics never goes away. As Tipple and Wellman (1991, 423) said of Kaufman's book, "It is doubtful that the author [were he writing in 1990] could focus exclusively on the internal workings of the organization and get an accurate picture." One could reasonably doubt that that was the case in 1960 either, the year of Kaufman's book. When Kaufman discussed the fraud and bribery that characterized the General Land Office before it became part of the U.S.

Forest Service, he did not mention the mining and timber interests, whose political power was felt in Congress, or the political struggle of the conservationists and progressives who pushed for change. The problem in the General Land Office, in Kaufman's telling, was laxity, centralization, authoritarian management, and poor leadership by men unfamiliar with conditions in the field. Hence, one would readily surmise that the problem was about competence and not about politics or power. Professional forestry was the answer. Kaufman is not necessarily wrong to frame it this way; except that "professional forestry" was itself an intense political battle led by the indefatigable Gifford Pinchot and his political ally Theodore Roosevelt. Kaufman's book scarcely mentions the word *conservation* although this was the enabling value premise that got the organization going and one that continues to sustain it.

When Franklin Hough addressed a Chamber of Commerce committee regarding the condition of the Adirondack forests, he called for what the *New York Times* (1884) said was a broad, enlightened, and efficient system of forest management that would embrace the care of public woodlands, leading to profits and benefits from the preservation of their existing woodlands. The public policy issue was thus framed in terms of profits and benefits, to be sure, but also in terms of forest preservation. The value of preservation implied that the forests were valuable as an end in themselves; conservation was an instrumentally nuanced belief that use-value should be taken into account. Kaufman avoids saying anything important about the genesis or history, much less the political environment, of the U.S Forest Service, even though his own managerial thesis is imbued with politics. Decentralization (which Kaufman explicitly recognized as an ideological proposition) is indeed a contestable organizational proposal and remains so in recent years, with political implications for environmentalists as well as the organization and the forest rangers. For example, the *New York Times* quoted the president of the Defenders of Wildlife as complaining that "the bottom line is that this is a significant rollback of required protections for wildlife and habitat compared to what currently exists" (L. Kaufman 2011). The "this" at issue for environmentalists was the particular wording of management standards that deferred to local managers with respect to their implementation, leaving the size of buffer areas around rivers and streams unspecified, and, according to a program director for the Pew Environmental Groups, included a lot of "mays" and few "musts." Environmental groups were thus objecting to the decentralized practices of the U.S. Forest Service wherein local rangers have considerable sayso at the local level. A managerial narrative (of decentralized authority) is thus confronted by an environmental narrative that envisions restricting the discretion of forest rangers in the field. Established practice is at stake.

Narrowing the forestry narrative to operational concerns does not remove politics. Yet, the residual haze of the politics-administration dichotomy leaves public administration associating politics and policy with the legislative branch, while facts and rationality belong over here in the executive sphere named public administration. The public administration literature has long preferred facts and rationality to politics, even after this dubious preference was problematized. The way Waldo (1948/2007) put it is that the public administration literature expresses a philosophy. The ideal of science, the absence of poverty, the end of waste and corruption, and the elimination of extreme inequality characterize the good life, the *telos* of public administration. The decision criteria of this philosophy are facts and rationality, and the deciders should be the experts who possess technical competence. In this philosophy, more executive power would be a good thing. Waldo expressed some disagreement with this philosophy of the modern administrative state, which is hierarchical and authoritarian rather than democratic. But his incontrovertible point was simply that politics and political philosophy are not external to public administration.

Politics cannot be assumed away. The danger of doing so would be to reshape democracy to forms that are subservient to efficiency and rationality—precisely what Imas (2005) warned about in his extraordinary account of the Pinochet effect in Chile. For Spicer (2010) the acknowledgment of politics in public administration is not only an empirical fact but also a moral imperative—value conflict, pluralism, and adversarial argumentation are signs of healthy administrative practices. Critical of those in public administration who display contempt for constitutional democratic values, Rosenbloom (2000) appreciates the way that Congress sometimes delegates legislative authority to agencies, treating them as extensions of the legislative branch in terms of the procedures they use, and the congressional insistence that democratic-constitutional values, not only managerial values, are practiced. Nor did Stivers (1993) allow the field of public administration to get away with its political neutrality conceit. She showed how the efforts to justify and legitimize the administrative state by invoking images of expertise, leadership, and virtue have masked the problematic politics of these very images—never neutral and almost always gendered. Politics does not end when the implementation stage commences, as policy scholars know well (Pressman and Wildavsky 1973). There is no end of politics in public administration. Michel Foucault's work on governmental rationality makes vividly explicit the impact of managerial tactics and techniques on culture and society.

II. THE PROFOUNDLY POLITICAL TECHNIQUES OF PUBLIC ADMINISTRATION

Though it has not always been so, the purpose of government in modern history has become the welfare of the population (displacing sovereign power over the territory as the main aim). In modern times, the art of government entails caring for and controlling the population. Governmentality (that is, governmental rationality) encourages economic productivity and regulates the smooth and peaceable exchange of goods and services. By governmentality, Foucault (1979, 20) means: "The ensemble formed by the institutions, procedures, analyses, and reflections, the calculations and tactics that allow the exercise of this very specific albeit complex form of power, which has as its target population, as its principal form of knowledge political economy and as its essential technical means the apparatuses of security." The concept of population is central to the concept of governmentality. Governmentality operates differently from "the state," which presupposes a singular unity and functionality and concerns itself with territory and sovereignty. For Foucault (1979), the art of government now focuses on the population: rates of death and disease, scarcity and economic well-being, epidemics, rates of vaccination, mortality, marriage rates, and so on.

These tactics and techniques of governmentality are the very tactics and techniques of public administration—the prevailing managerial ideas and practices. These tactics and techniques blend with the dominant policy narrative at moments of policy implementation. The techniques include social statistics, cost-benefit analysis, program evaluation, rational decision protocols, outcomes assessment, privatization, and performance assessment, to name a few; all are aimed at the economic and social security of the population. Indeed, the problems of governmentality and the techniques of government have become the paramount political issue; perhaps the most important site for political contest and struggle.

Focusing on the problems of the population was not possible until the concept "population" became meaningfully interesting with respect to record keeping and statistics. The use of statistics, which had previously been operative within an administrative setting for purposes of monitoring the comings and goings in and out of the territory, "gradually reveals that population has its own regularities, its own rate of death, of diseases, its cycles of scarcity, etc. . . . [S]tatistics shows also that the domain of population involves a range of intrinsic, aggregate effects and that its phenomena, such for instance as the great epidemics, and the spiral of labor and wealth, are irreducible to the dimension of the family" (Foucault 1979, 17). Abandoning the family, which is to say the household, as the fundamental unit of society enabled the individual to emerge as the unit of analysis, with population serving as the aggregation of them. Aspects of the population are quantifiable through statistics. The population thus becomes the thing with needs, though the population itself may be ignorant of the things being done on its behalf. The individuals who constitute the population, regardless of their aspirations, are the new targets of the instruments of government. This was a new art of government, informed by new tactics and techniques.

Discipline, too, became an objective of governmental techniques (Foucault

1994). Deviance became medicalized as new classifications of disease arose, most conspicuously in the field of psychiatry. The social sciences gave rise to multiple classification schemes, which in turn presented control possibilities, including the possibility of containing segments of the population. Foucault (1994, 326) took particular notice of "dividing practices." Taking care of the population meant dividing off the lepers, the poor, and the insane. These divided-off elements of the population were relocated to hospitals or other asylums; the sick were separated from the healthy, the criminals from the good boys. This was a specific technique in the new science of government. The technique has advanced to the point where standard deviations can be calculated, norms can be established, and each individual can be precisely described in terms of distance from the norm on any measurable variable. According to Foucault (1995, 190–191), "These small techniques of notation, of registration, of constituting files, of arranging facts in columns and tables that are so familiar to us now, were of decisive importance in the epistemological 'thaw' of the sciences of the individual."

Governmental rationality is, hence, a form of knowledge that carries with it a form of power. The tactics and techniques of government are far from apolitical in their effects or their applications, yet, the cultural effects of public administration's practices and techniques mostly escape notice. Politics extends further than policy deliberation; culture and habitus—and the practices taken for granted—are also political terrain. Those practices, techniques, and tactics that are presupposed to constitute neutral expertise (or best practices) have a profoundly political role in stabilizing society, reinforcing the status quo, caring for the population, and controlling it.

So far in this chapter, the political has reasserted itself in public management. Politics is understood, though, not in a utilitarian who-gets-what calculation that deploys the utility-maximizing individual as the unit of analysis, but rather as a matter of changing social practices. Interests, in a narrative approach, are conceptualized ideographically, a concept associated with calculations of instrumental gain.

III. INTERESTS AS A SOCIAL CONSTRUCTION

Policy scholars sometimes write about *material interests* or *objective interests,* as if an observer could stand outside all narratives and figure out what is best for someone. From an ideographic perspective, the invocation of *material interests,* like the invocation of *objective science,* seems to presuppose an objective Archimedean standpoint—a view from nowhere. In discourse theory, interests are but perceptions of interests—perceptions as determined by cultural habitus and massaged according to the circumstances. The difference—between realist conceptions of interests and the present discursive conception of interests—matters because "material interests" imposes a standard that purports to reside outside of the discourse. "Material interests," as proposed in the scholarly literature, attempts to trump other claims, using well-hewn tactics such as "false consciousness" to distinguish between perceptions of interests (that are dubious) and material interests (that are *real* and prelinguistic). This maneuver never really works because "material interests" is itself a socially constructed category lacking the denotative prestige it wants to presuppose for itself. Calling an interest *material* as opposed to *perceived* solves nothing; instead, it opens up a redundant conversation on perspectivism, a conversation that the modifier "perceived" has already implicitly acknowledged. Demonstrating the materiality of a particular interest entails pitting one narrative against another, and, in the process, its objectivity reveals itself as perspectival.

One effect of the "interests" ideograph is to warrant *gain* as a proper motivation for conduct. More generally, "interests" invites the decentered subject to identify with (that is, associate him/herself with) some proposals or aspirations and not with others. In discourse theory, not even *money* is a material interest, but rather a highly sedimented cultural reification. Money is a highly successful, meaning-laden symbol that is understood in an extraordinarily wide range of contexts and practices. The ideograph *money*, embedded in a readerly narrative about prosperity, has achieved such dominance that the phrase "material interests objectively understood" can resonate throughout society, narrative theory notwithstanding. Without attempting to deconstruct *money* here, a narrative approach would appreciate that cultures did not always make use of money. Polanyi (1944/2001) reminded us that barter practices, as well as the market practices that followed, are embedded in culture and society. Interests, too, is a culturally embedded construct.

Interests must be performed if they are to count as social action. Median voter models, public choice political economy, and the rational choice school of institutional sociology have generated many examples of this type of performance. The performance of interests entails the actions that are inspired by one's understanding of one's interests. Interests (or some synonymously functioning telos such as goal or objective) presuppose an instrumentally rational orientation to social action. It is tempting to assume that all public policy discourse is of this sort, and that all arguments are strategically crafted political manipulations. (But there are other orientations toward social action, including habit, values, imitation, and emotions.) Purposive spin, propaganda, and manipulative marketing should not be ruled out in policy discourse; these are instances of performed interests. Ideography can itself be subordinated to instrumental performances, as the marketing profession has amply demonstrated. If media conglomerates, power elites, or ordinary citizens understand the distribution and production of particular ideographs to be in their interests, one can expect them to promote more of such ideographs. The political playing field of policy discourse is bursting with purposive attempts motivated by perceived interests to reconfigure the symbolic associations of some issue or question up for public discussion. But, even so, the narrative approach understands the concept of interests, whatever ideas and aspirations a culture links it with, to be a culturally specific social construction.

Having brought politics into the picture in several different ways in sections I, II, and III, section IV proposes a discursive interpretation of political disputes. Political contestation comes at moments of impasse, where old practices are challenged or new practices are introduced, when it becomes evident that something meaningful is at issue.

IV. STATUS QUO AND CHANGE

Regularized (institutionalized) social practices generate social order and cultural stability. Public policy is often itself an attempt to marshal order and regularity for a society. Public policy making explicitly reveals knowledge, rationales, and operations that justify, explain, and legitimate the prevailing regime of social practices. Indeed, these are the functions of policy discourse. Proposals to change those same legitimately established practices are also justified and legitimated through a discursive policy process. By legitimating and establishing social practices, public policy discourse contributes to governing by weaving the raw materials of culture—signifiers and ideographs—into coherent narratives and social order. Public policy discourse has a unique role in legitimating social interventions.

Ubiquitous contestation among ideographs and narratives—some at the macro level (e.g., the antigovernment, antiregulatory narrative versus the climate change narrative) and most at the level of daily practice (such as the decentralized mode of operations at the U.S. Forest Service)—generates a volatile background of opportunities for potential change. Public administration is vulnerable to change from both within and without. Changes in the political and social environment can influence practices inside the organization. Internally, challenges to operational procedures are as common as a technology upgrade. Tensions between centralization and decentralization, staff analysts and line managers, the lawyers' ways versus the accountants' ways (to name but one possible occupational conflict) permeate organizational culture. If innovation and change are to occur inside an organization, there must be politics (Pfeffer 1992).

Politics comes into focus at moments of impasse. At the point of impasse the status quo has become problematic. In most situations, one thinks and acts similarly to the way one has thought and acted in the past. However, some physical and social situations call for new responses. The problems that old practices were designed to solve may have disappeared or changed. Or instrumentally better ways and means are now available. The old ways may have become emotionally untenable. It could be that one's identifications and values have changed, and the old ways are no longer acceptable. A new and different image of success, or a new ideograph, may have entered one's consciousness. An impasse may take many forms, including changed condition, disgust with some aspect of current practice, policy learning, technological advances, or a new opportunity. In any case, the old ways no longer satisfy the current demands of the situation. Once established and institutionalized, the old ways seemed like second nature. But they cannot have been the only way to do things. We have reached an *impasse*. Hope for amelioration must now confront the anxiety of destabilization when habits and known practices are at risk of being undermined.

Isolating the moment of impasse faces difficulties similar to those confronted by Simon (1976, 221) when he tried to nail down the moment of decision:

> It should be perfectly apparent that almost no decision made in an organization is the task of a single individual. Even though the final responsibility for taking a particular action rests with some definite person, we shall always find, in studying the manner in which this decision was reached, that its various components can be traced through the formal and informal channels of communication to many individuals who have participated in forming its premises. When all of these components have been identified, it may appear that the contribution of the individual who made the formal decision was a minor one, indeed.

There are broad decisions regarding the content of the organization's work that cannot be systematically formalized because of contingencies such as the technology in use, efficiency considerations, subject-matter competency, and on-the-job social relations—including the different values and rationalities operative in different parts of the organization. If rational calculation were all there is to it, decisions would be easy. But easy or difficult, one person's decision is but the next person's informational input that may be discarded, reinterpreted, faithfully enacted, or actively opposed.

The concreteness of "the decision" is illusory because the next moment may make it malleable; "impasse" presupposes malleability, anticipating movement rather than fixity. *Impasse* is unlike Simon's *decision* in that it makes no presuppositions that an administrator is facing the impasse (though it could be an administrator), no automatic separation of the relevant components into facts and values, no presupposition of cooperation, and no reliance on a categorical distinction between formal and informal channels (though these associations may be relevant). But moments of impasse are like Simon's composite decision in that they both entail complex association and interaction processes.

The situational contingency of ostensibly permanent social structures is exposed at such moments, revealing institutionalized yet changeable social practices. A moment of impasse represents a potential for conflict, as sedimented practices and established narratives seek to reinforce or defend themselves. Change does not necessarily follow—but it might. So in addition to the usual suspects who resist change—elites who benefit from the status quo, the capitalists who want to continue to exploit labor, and so on—there is a general resistance to changing the narratives and practices that we have grown comfortable with. Action on behalf of change accompanies successful symbolic redescription and the rearranging of stable narratives.

Everyday life tends toward the habitual, and most of us like it that way. We do not want to have to renegotiate each next moment from scratch any more than we would like to reconstruct a new persona every day. When we walk past someone in the hallway, it is customary to say something like "Good morning, how are you?" This might elicit a "Fine, thank you. And you?" "Fine." This banal conversation is interesting only because of all the things it is not. The behaviors that have been exhibited by humans when they approach one another range from indifference, to beheading with a machete, to robbery, shooting, and worse. The banality of order can be comforting. We like to know what to expect from one another. Doing everything differently every day would be disorienting and anxiety generating. There are regularities in our lives because of the patterns generated through daily practice and through stable ideography arranged into well-understood narratives. At work or at sport, we carry with us certain expectations of others and bring knowledge of the routines we learned yesterday or last year or in childhood. This predictability of everyday practices enables long-term cooperative projects and makes the world seem like an orderly place. Political judgment comes into play not when status quo practices suffice, but when they are contested in some way.

At moments of impasse, the direction of change may be unpredictable. Consider, for example, the Sagebrush Rebellion, a reaction to the environmental practices taking place through federal land policy in the 1970s. Federal policy had changed so that public lands previously used solely for grazing were not just for grazing any more. Outdoor recreation had become a legitimate use of public lands. Moreover, public land was increasingly designated as "wilderness area," which restricted its use. "And since a key management principle for wilderness was to preserve its primitive condition, 'any economic use of the area such as the grazing of livestock that may exist at the time of its establishment should be discontinued as soon as practicable and equitable and no further commercial utilization of the resources should be allowed' [quoting the U.S. Congress, Outdoor Recreation Resources Review Commission]" (Cawley 1993, 23–24). Sagebrush Rebels, operating within a completely different narrative perspective, were advocates of commodity production on public lands and opponents of preservation efforts—hence the impasse. "The Sagebrush Rebellion appears to have been an authentic political movement deriving support from a diverse group of people who believed that federal land management policies had become overly responsive to environmental preservation values" (Cawley 1993, 14). In opposition, the Sagebrush Rebellion tapped into an anti-government-regulation narrative, a states' rights narrative, and an economic-development narrative with respect to public lands. The Sagebrush Rebellion succeeded in putting their impasse on the policy agenda, calling into question the environmental practices that had been put into place.

Yet something had been happening to the Sagebrush narrative as it was being massaged in Washington, D.C. While Secretary of the Interior James Watt apparently subscribed to the implicit Sagebrush agenda, a slightly different narrative gained traction in the Reagan administration and among allies in Congress to hijack the states' rights platform. Under the ideograph *privatization,* sale of public land to private interests was being proposed. According to Cawley (1993, 124), "the privatization initiative did not emerge from the Interior Department" but from other probusiness economic policy voices. "Contrary to the view prevailing at the time, privatization was neither a goal of the Sagebrush Rebellion nor part of Interior Secretary James Watt's agenda. Instead, privatization advocates were attempting to use the controversies surrounding the Sagebrush Rebellion to advance their own agenda." As it turned out, the sale of public lands did not pass Congress, but the terms of the debate were, nonetheless, moving further toward a promarket, antigovernment narrative.

A moment of impasse, then, is an opportunity for new signifiers and ideographs to gain ascendance, by latching onto a narrative that becomes dominant, or at least has the potential to become dominant. A narrative's success at upsetting the status quo does not necessarily imply that it will become the new order. Nonetheless, impasses are moments of political conflict in the symbolic environment, where institutionalized ideography and practice are called into question, and history gets a chance to move. Impasses make problematic both ideographic identifications and established practices. Practice and language change together or stabilize together in a symbiotic relationship.

In sociology, status quo ways have been described as habitus (e.g., Bourdieu 1977). In the next section, the narrative approach regards habitus as a readerly text, which is to say, social practices that are performed as second-nature habit.

V. HABITUS

Policy implementation is a sufficiently vague term for capturing the ambiguous imprecision of transforming policy decisions into social action. There is no automatic mechanism for calming the turbulence that awaits the institutionalization process. Moreover, even well-established government agencies only *seem* far removed from the kind of uncertainty and controversy that accompanies newly formed institutions such as the U.S. Forest Service of the early 1900s or the Environmental Protection Agency of the early 1970s. Yet, despite the potential for political volatility, some governmental organizations have endured over a long period of time and have regularized their practices. A culture of regularity and mutual expectation—where acquired responses, dispositions, practices, and behaviors come to seem like second nature—can be described as habitus. Habitus for Bourdieu (1977) is the production of the commonsense world. It is the continuous reinforcement that organizational actors receive from expressing their normalized experience. Habitus is much like the sedimented habitual comportments (Fox and Miller 1995) that regularize, normalize, and naturalize customs and conventional ways of going about things. Habitus could be likened to a readerly text. As a sort of collective mastery of a common code—red means stop, for example—habitus is a precondition for the coordination of practices.

Habitus also serves as an alternative theory to the "prison-industrial complex" policy narrative purportedly explaining the continued war on drugs, discussed in appendix 1. Who gains from the war on drugs? "Critical observers attempting to describe the construction and operation of a thug state infrastructure have coined provocative terms to alert our attention" (Richards and Avery 2000, 52). Vivid images include *carceral archipelago, American gulag,* the *vice-industrial complex,* the *prison-industrial complex,* the *criminal justice–industrial complex,* the *perpetual incarceration machine,* the *correctional-industrial complex,* and the *drug war–industrial complex.* The idea is that local police departments, federal prosecutors, the Drug Enforcement Administration, prison guards, and other public entities need the war on drugs for their continued funding. Lack of success in stemming the demand or supply of illegal drugs is beside the point. But as Bourdieu (1977, 80) put it, "Without habitus, everything is the conscious coordination of a conspiracy, a naïve artificialism that recognizes no other principle unifying a group action. The immanent law is only habitus, affecting us all since early upbringing." With habitus, one can understand that the prison guards, the police, and the drug enforcement officials are merely performing the same ritual they performed yesterday. Habitus thus counters conspiracy as a competing account for the continued war on drugs.

Habitus may also be conceptualized as a dynamic and ongoing performance of a culture's archival ideography. Organizations, conceptualized as sites of habitus, "are suspended in a web of values, norms, rules, beliefs, and taken-for-granted assumptions that are at least partially of their own making" (Barley and Tolbert 1997, 93). This is the sort of institutionalization that can occur when a long-forgotten policy narrative becomes implemented and institutionalized. The institutional habitus generates unexamined regularity. For Bourdieu (1977, 79), "It is because subjects do not, strictly speaking, know what they are doing that what they do has more meaning than they know. The habitus is the universalizing mediation which causes an individual agent's practices, without either explicit reason or signifying intent, to be none the less 'sensible' and 'reasonable.'" For Bourdieu (1977), the unconscious is the forgetting of history as history fades into habitus—history adopted into a sort of second nature that only *appears* to be a static institution. The unconscious allows institutional participants to draw on their past histories without a whole lot of effort. Instead of static institutions and self-interested conspirators, then, we have regularized, habitual, perhaps unconscious performance.

Habitus implies a deeply embedded narrative, a set of predispositions and sensibilities, and an almost unthinking form of social action. Tradition and habit inform social practice, privileging status quo arrangements by shielding them from the domain of political contestation, by taking such arrangements for granted. In making choices we typically go with the typical; the convention is to behave in a conventional manner; habitual action is my usual habit—though all these could be otherwise.

Chapter 4 reaffirmed the political potential inherent in everyday practices while appreciating that sedimented habits do not willingly announce themselves as practices ripe for change. Yet, even presumably neutral tactics and techniques, such as statistical analysis, have profound social and cultural effects. In other words, the everyday tactics and techniques of public administration would be interpreted as a writerly text rather than a readerly text, were one to focus on the contestability of such practices. The moment of such contest would be considered an impasse, when latent politics becomes visible politics. It is perhaps customary to imagine impasses as traceable to interests, which could manifest themselves as goals or values. Less obvious analytically than instrumentally, rational social action or value-rational social action is social action inspired by imitation. In chapter 5, I will discuss imitation, repetition, and replication as a mode of evolutionary change whose politics are subtle. Association returns to center stage, not exclusively as connotation, but as a network of relationships, ideas, practices, and objects. The focus on networks of associations leads to a reconceptualization of social structures—as effects rather than causes. At the everyday level, social action is performed in symbiotic networks of meanings, connotations, objects, practices, and narratives.

5
Narrative Performance

Before we get to the performance of symbiotic networks of meanings, connotations, objects, practices, and narratives, some advance work will be necessary.
Values, habits, feelings, and instrumental rationality have all been gathered into
ideographs at various points in the book thus far. In addition to these orientations to social action, chapter 1 mentioned the category *imitation;* this chapter
returns to that topic as a preface to an evolutionary approach to policy change
that relies on symbiotic associations for both repetition of practices and changes
to them.

I. IMITATION AND COOPERATION

Weber (1978) organized his social action typology with a reason-giving individual actor in mind, as noted in chapter 1. But because of his emphasis on the
self-conscious orientation to one's social milieu, one category that Weber excluded from his schema was *imitation* as proposed by Gabriel Tarde (1903). Imitation did not meet Weber's criteria of social action. Though Weber had read
Tarde and considered adding imitation as a fifth category, he decided against
it because there would be "no meaningful orientation to the actor imitated"
(Weber 1978, 23). Social action would be purely reactive were imitation to be included in Weber's view, as imitation is not meaningfully determined. It would

not be an acceptable reason for action for Weber's purposive social actor. However, this limitation on the social actor's reason for acting would not work if Weber's autonomous, intentional individual were instead a decentered subject. Studies in emotion and social interaction are suggestive of the social implications of imitation.

Psychologists have noticed a tendency for people "to mimic and synchronize their movements with the facial expressions, voices, postures, movements, and instrumental behaviors of others" (Hatfield, Cacioppo, and Rapson 1994, 10; also see 47). To take a simple example, smiling often elicits smiles in others. Emotional signals, such as smiling, can trigger automatic nervous system activity and other behavioral manifestations, indicating the possible spread of an emotional state. This research raises the possibility that emotions do not necessarily come from deep within one's soul but may be transported interpersonally.

In the age of the Internet and mass marketing, concepts such as imitation, replication, mimesis, emotional contagion, and "gone viral" deserve recognition as ways of stimulating the performance of social action. The decentered subject is exposed to the inscriptions left by imitation and replication even if the robust, autonomous individual is not. Things that repeat themselves fascinated Tarde (1903, 6), and he distinguished between the sort of repetition observed in (1) the chemical, physical, and astronomical worlds, named *vibratory repetition;* (2) biological organic reproduction, named *hereditary repetition;* and (3) resemblances of a social origin, such as custom imitation, fashion imitation, sympathy imitation, obedience imitation, precept imitation, education imitation, naïve imitation, or deliberate imitation—different forms of *imitative repetition.* Resemblances and repetitions are the necessary themes of difference and variation that exist in all phenomena, he theorized. A narrative approach would leave Tarde's thesis of vibratory repetition, which applied to chemistry, physics, and astronomy, for knowledgeable others to judge. Meanwhile, his hereditary repetition seems derivative of Darwin. Imitative repetition, however, was both an original contribution to social thought and relevant to social action. Tarde (1903, 191) extended the scope of imitation broadly: "Red tape and administrative routine, the etiquette of government, increase day by day with differentiation in government. Architecture requires its followers to become more and more servile in the repetition of the consecrated types that are for the time being in favor. This is true also of music. Painting also requires its servants to reproduce with more and more photographic exactness the models of nature or tradition."

Tarde interpreted many things—from obedience to buying furniture to repeating something from the newspaper—as another iteration of imitation. Indeed, "[U]nless man in society is inventing, a rare occurrence, or unless he is following impulses which are of a purely organic origin, likewise a rarer and rarer occurrence, he is always, in act or thought, imitating" (Tarde 1903, 391). To the degree that humans are social, they are essentially imitative. As Hoffer (2006, 17) mused, "When people are free to do as they please, they usually imitate each other."

Like imitation, replication does not require teleology or purposeful intent; accident plus selection are about all that there is. In Darwinian terms, symbolizations evolve and adapt to their environments, which are made up of other symbolizations also striving to replicate. It only retrospectively seems that each species (or symbolization) had a purposive survival strategy. In the words of Dewey (1997, 9), "The classic notion of species carried with it the idea of purpose." Dewey (1997, 10) challenged the way philosophers generated universal principles based on this supposed purposefulness: "Since this purposive regulation is not visible to the senses, it follows [for these philosophers] that it must be an ideal or rational force." While Dewey's criticism of this anti-Darwinian teleology in philosophy was astute, it may not have occurred to him that the evolution of language might be as contingent, irrational, and accidental as biological evolution. However, Dawkins, like Tarde, made use of the generalizability of the replication idea, this time by drawing an analogy between gene self-interest (a biological phenomenon) and *meme* self-interest (a cultural phenomenon). "Genes are replicated, copied from parent to offspring down the generations. A meme is, by analogy, anything that replicates itself from brain to brain, via any available means of copying" (Dawkins 1989, 302). "The analogy between genetic and memetic evolution starts to get interesting when we apply our lesson of 'the selfish cooperator.' Memes, like genes, survive in the presence of certain other memes. A mind can become prepared, by the presence of certain memes, to be receptive to particular other memes. . . . The right way to see it is in terms of mutually assisting memes, each providing an environment which favors the others" (306).

Cooperation and mutual assistance are novel ways to think of genetic survival; in social networks, such associative concepts are not novel at all. By selfish cooperator, Dawkins means that successful genes—the ones that survive— must be able to flourish in an environment that consists of the other genes found in the species. Genes of a species get selected because they are good at cooperating with each other, to the extent that cooperation is instrumental to survival. The narrative approach of this book utilizes concepts such as signs, ideographs, and narratives (and not memes), but Dawkins's concept of replication meshes with Tarde's concept of imitation on the dynamic of cooperation. An idea that can associate (by similarity, difference, rhyme, emotional response, and so on) with an already existing sign, ideograph, or narrative has more likelihood of becoming a successful idea (that is, it survives) than one that lacks associative resonance. Resonant ideas associate with other signs, ideographs, and narratives to warrant action. The transformation of symbolizations into practice is thus an evolutionary process.

The idea that language evolves is widespread in communications theory. Evolutionary metaphors abound in the public policy literature as well. John (2003) authored a cautionary discussion of evolutionary approaches found in Baumgartner and Jones (1993), Kingdon (1984), Sabatier and Jenkins-Smith (1993), and Dawkins (1989). His chief concern was that the causal mechanisms of random variation and natural selection are not necessarily transferable to social science research. However, the narrative approach of this book shifts the unit of analysis from individuals and groups to signs, ideographs, and narratives. From the perspective of the sign, the environment of human communication performs the selection function. Most evolutionary approaches envision incremental change; in the narrative approach, signs evolve to connote ideography. Recall the way that roses come to connote passion. The evolutionary staying power of the ideograph is strengthened further when it is appropriated into, say, a romance narrative.

However, the dynamic of successful change of narrative is not always a mere incremental shift in interpretation, but sometimes requires, in addition, a *punctuation* of the long-enduring stability enforced by status quo institutions and habits of mind. Jones and Baumgartner (2005) borrowed the evolutionary metaphor *punctuated equilibrium* to describe the drag imposed by status quo institutions. Settled equilibrium successfully prevents policy change—until a major punctuation to the discourse is able to overcome the forces of friction that had been resisting change. The drag of deeply sedimented and powerful ideographs ensconced in narratives can be overcome sometimes by sufficiently resonant alternatives. These alternatives already must have gathered enough momentum to shake the deep roots of established habitus and their reinforcing ideography. Jones and Baumgartner (2005) would describe the policy upshot of destabilizing events, images, and ideographs as an *intrusion*. An intrusion can dislocate old policy-making equilibriums. "An issue intrudes when a problem is severe and when the signal indicating the severity of that problem is weighted heavily" (Jones and Baumgartner 2005, 226). Intrusions can be brought on by events and crises, but this need not be the case. "[M]obilization cascades, lobbying campaigns, and the search for new and potentially popular new issues make such dynamics a permanent feature of the American policy process" (83).

When terms such as *equilibrium* displace terms such as *organizational structure* in signifying stability, the constitution of institutions is called into question, as is the presupposition of permanence. Punctuations and windows of opportunity are moments when institutional change is imminent. In the next section, the narrative approach takes the next step in further detailing policy evolution at the level of practice.

II. STRUCTURE RECONSIDERED

In the scholarly literature the term *institution* traditionally connoted fixity, structure, and stability. Since Giddens (1984), however, there has been a growing appreciation that institutions are constituted by the regularity of practices. The reiteration of practices does not happen automatically. Practices, associations, and connotations can be enduring, and can seem rigid like a structure. Yet, terms such as *practices, connotations,* and *associations,* unlike terms such as *structure* and *system,* are better able to train attention on the continual need to reinforce the so-called structure—that is, to perform the regularity. The regularity is not structured fixity so much as a daily performance of ritual. Stable fixed structures are not static; instead, the order implied by such terms must be regularly re-created, even if those re-creations have come to be habitually or unconsciously performed and even if today's repetition is not an exact replica of yesterday's.

A. Performing the Narrative

E. E. Schattschneider was attuned to the importance of politics in changing the status quo. "Organization is itself a mobilization of bias. Some issues are organized into politics while others are organized out," according to Schattschneider (1960, 69). In the narrative approach, this idea must be taken seriously—that organizations (specifically public administration institutions) emerge from a mobilization of political sentiment. Political sentiment is expressed via narratives; as political sentiment changes, meanings and practices are subject to change over time. Dominant narratives and institutionalized practices can be rewritten and reinterpreted or altered.

Such malleability led Selznick (1996) to articulate the concern that the fragile foundation of institutional stability and integration is constituted by nothing more solid than social entanglements and commitments. Yet, even situational entanglements, Selznick (1996, 271) allows, can be rather constraining: "Most of what we do in everyday life is mercifully free and reversible. But when actions touch important issues and salient values or when they are embedded in networks of interdependence, options are more limited. Institutionalization constrains conduct in two main ways: by bringing it within a normative order and by making it hostage to its own history." Those two constraints, the normative order and history, are embedded in the readerly text, in the now-unspoken narrative that reinforces established practices of the habitus. To change practices, one must raise the unspoken narrative back into consciousness in order to displace it. Displacement of institutionalized practices begins with a rewriting of the once-readerly narrative or the writing of a new one.

Once the new narrative becomes dominant or sufficiently salient (not necessarily a simple or short-term process), new social action displaces old practices. Rachel Carson rewrote the narrative of DDT, to take a grand example of changing a narrative and, hence, social practices. Her book begins with a fable, and the reader is invited to imagine an idyllic town whose roads are lined with laurel, alder, ferns, and wildflowers. Foxes bark and deer silently cross the fields in the morning mist. There are birds and fish. But then, like an evil spell, a strange blight changes everything. Farmers' families become ill, and unexplained deaths, especially among the children, are on the rise. Where did the birds go? No bees, no chicks; unusually small pig litters. The vegetation is brown and withered and the streams are empty of fish. Is this some enemy action? Some witchcraft? No. "The people had done it to themselves" (Carson 1962, 3). Values, emotions, and ideographic connotations are interposed in the fable. Carson then proceeds to lay out a passionate argument, albeit with more scholarly distance, about modernity's impact on the environment, most particularly about the negative effects of the pesticide DDT. The book documents lawsuits by beekeepers over aerial spraying of DDT and the loss of salmon from four streams in British Columbia. Young salmon were "almost completely annihilated" (138). And there is a call to action: "To assume that we must resign ourselves to turning our waterways into rivers of death is to follow the counsel of despair and defeatism" (138). And there are sensible criticisms of managerial practices: "The gypsy moth programs were marked by many acts of irresponsibility. Because the spray planes were paid by the gallon rather than by the acre there was no effort to be conservative, and many properties were sprayed not once but several times" (160–161).

The reader would not discern this from Carson's account, but DDT was once highly regarded as an effective insect killer that drastically reduced the incidence of typhus and malaria among U.S. troops during World War II. By the 1960s, it was becoming evident that DDT could accumulate in birds and fish and kill them, as Carson pointed out. But by 1970 nothing had been done to reduce or halt DDT spraying. Brody (1969) reported that DDT had actually survived the scathing indictment by Carson and that into the late 1960s the chemical industry continued to produce hundreds of millions of pounds of DDT per year. And yet miniscule amounts of DDT, detectable by gas chromatograph technology, could kill birds and fish (Higdon 1969). Concentrations as low as two parts per trillion were enough to cause problems, especially in birds. Biologists were able to detect concentrations of DDT in plankton, which were eaten by fish, and in worms that ate fallen leaves, which were then eaten by birds. This process, known as biological magnification, eventually led to bird kills and fish kills. Scientific accounts of this process were reported in newspaper articles (e.g., Lyons 1967). In a research journal, Woodwell, Wurster, and Isaacson (1967, 821) reported that the "highest concentrations [of DDT] occurred in scavenging and carnivorous fish and birds, although birds had 10 to 100 times more than fish. These concentrations approach those in animals dying from DDT poisoning, which suggests that many natural populations in this area [south shore of Long Island] are now being affected."

Biological magnification is particularly problematic for birds of prey that feed on fish (Brody 1969). Reports of drastic reductions in bald eagles' nests around Lake Michigan seemed like confirmatory evidence to conservationists. Indeed, in 1969 the Michigan agricultural commission banned DDT on the basis of evidence that Coho salmon were contaminated with excessive amounts of DDT. As the *New York Times* (1969, 15) reported: "It is the first of the 50 states to take such action. The State Agriculture Commission voted to cancel all registrations for the sale of the controversial pesticide. Soaring concentrations of DDT in the pesticide dieldrin has turned up in the fat of salmon, whitefish, trout and perch."

The fish were of important economic consequence in Michigan, especially the popular Coho salmon, much sought by sport fishermen. "A few dead robins or eagle eggs without shells are one thing, but $100-million worth of tourist trade is another, and that's what seemed to be at stake" (Higdon 1969, 34).

As might be expected, there was pushback from the DDT manufacturers. DDT was not only a cheap pesticide to use—its persistence made frequent applications unnecessary—it was also a popular moneymaker. To protect this profitable business, the five American DDT manufacturers . . . have organized a task force to defend their products against what they call "emotional" attacks. The DDT task force provided a number of witnesses at the hearings in Wisconsin. They testified that DDT does not harm humans and warned that its complete elimination would leave the state vulnerable to outbreaks of such diseases as encephalitis. (Higdon 1969, 6)

Hence, the sense of preserving and protecting the wild for its innate worth as nature, as John Muir and Rachel Carson argued, was buttressed by the threat to the bald eagle (often referred to as the American eagle, thus connoting patriotic imagery), the threat to tourism and recreational fishing, and the credibility of scientific findings. William Ruckelshaus, first head of the Environmental Protection Agency (EPA), selected the DDT issue as a way of establishing the credibility of the new agency. He did not want environmentalism to be marginalized, dismissed, or ignored. "So when [some American industrialists] decided to confront me or the agency, it was simple to take them on. We couldn't have invented any better antagonist for the purpose of showing that this was serious business, that the agency was serious about its mission" (Ruckelshaus 1993, 5). In 1972, 10 years after the publication of *Silent Spring,* the EPA banned the synthetic pesticide DDT.

The process of problematizing certain social practices or social conditions involves a struggle—to deem *this* problem as normatively worthy of contestation, *this* impasse as deserving of wider attention. The "this" does not have to be a large culture-wide issue, such as the one that Carson raised. The problem could be a seemingly trivial managerial concern. In environmental agencies such as the EPA and U.S. Forest Service, management is highly political. Though we may attribute permanency, structure, and social order to the term *institution,* we are usually discussing changeable vagaries such as norms and customs, behaviors and purposes, social constructions and period-piece artifacts.

B. Endorsing the Status Quo

Institutions can be viewed as an accumulation of precedents, akin to the dead hand of the past, but they can also suggest a sort of solidarity in the sharing of a legacy. Gueras and Garofalo (2005, 18) portray their institutional perspective as an ethical stance, a form of public stewardship. While institutional maintenance may seem a mundane chore, they argue, it can also be a way of rising to something worthwhile and enduring, but without engaging in self-flattery. There is much in common between this view of institutions and Heclo's (2008, 107) view that "because institutions are an inheritance of valued purpose and moral obligation, they constitute socially ordered groundings for human life. Such grounding in a normative field implicates the lives of individuals and collectivities in a lived-out social reality." However, Heclo is not content to merely praise established institutional thinking; he labels change-oriented narratives as socially disembodied utopianism (207). As a general proposition, when stated outside of context, Heclo's statement tends to favor the status quo. For him, innovation is not necessarily better; submission to authority is not necessarily worse. Inherited values are not necessarily cultural oppressions. These are truisms, of course, but Heclo's move also naturalizes the status quo. The demur, from the narrative approach, would be that both tradition and change have in common that they are constituted by narrative, and the criteria for judging one narrative superior to another are matters for political contestation. The competition among ideographs and narratives does not imply that the best narrative wins; only that the winning narrative has won for the time being. Unseating the established narrative is a difficult political task, particularly when the narrative has settled into habitual institutional practice. The status quo has habitus on its side, but habitus can and perhaps should change.

The subjective effect of habitual practice may relieve the anxiety of daily chaos, of one-dang-thing-after-another, but widely legitimate narratives also contribute to social order as social actors learn to expect certain actions from one another. That is, Heclo is not necessarily wrong in favoring the status quo, but it depends on the situation, and the values that are at stake—the narrative that is being preserved. Social order is a performance of habitus and narrative dominance, a narrative enacted perhaps without much rational thought. The habitual conventions that accompany institutionalization enable coordination, cooperation, and fulfillment of mutual expectations, to be sure. The narrative thus entrenched is often able to dismiss its challengers as idealisms, as Heclo (2008) does, even though the dominant, institutionalized narrative, too, is a performed idealism—but with history and therefore habitus on its side.

Dominant institutionalized narratives will take defensive and offensive maneuvers against challengers that seek to displace the dominant one from its privileged position. Sedimented practices and established narratives dominate by selecting in and selecting out cooperating/competing ideographs and practices.

C. Selection: Inclusion and Exclusion

The institutionalized narrative is in a favorable position to criticize alternative views and stories and to generate reinforcing ones. The case illustrations of recreational drug policy and environmental policy offer some hints about how selection works. In a simple example, the EPA came up against sedimented habitus in its early days. The U.S. Department of Commerce, the Federal Power Commission, and the Office of Management and Budget resisted EPA efforts to impose new regulations on corporations (Landy, Roberts, and Thomas 1994, 33). These resisting agencies operated under different narratives supported by different constituencies. These already-established institutions performed a selection function with respect to the inclusion and exclusion of both symbolic ideography and social practices around issues of regulation. Deeply embedded, established practices of the habitus, though malleable, will also serve as gatekeeper to emergent or potential practices, enabling some and inhibiting others. Resistance by established institutionalized practices can influence the developmental process of an emerging practice by potentially modifying the meaning of any of the raw materials of policy discourse, which is to say by intervening and altering the connotations that inform social action.

Meanwhile, competing narratives do not necessarily disappear or vacate the field when the dominant narrative apparently wins the day; they carry on in the background, in the cultural archives, despite a setback. Moreover, competing narratives can assert themselves in reaction to the attempts to put into practice the winning narrative—as happened at both the U.S. Forest Service and the EPA when regulated industries fought back against the regulation of natural resources and pollution. There is potential volatility throughout the implementation process. But the dominant narrative, once it is institutionalized, defines the status quo way of understanding problems in its domain. Defending against new concepts, alternate story lines, and competing narratives is always a difficult task, but it is made an easier task when undertaken from a stabilized institutional perch.

When the Federal Bureau of Narcotics was established in 1930, there had been 30 years of society wondering aloud about the ready availability of alcohol, heroin, morphine, and cocaine. The Prohibition Unit in the U.S. Treasury Department was already well established and housed a narcotics division within the unit, charged to enforce the 1916 Harrison Act, which was a revenue act. The more institutionalized into practice the antidrug discourse became, the better positioned was the narrative to control the conversation, influence the meaning of signs and ideographs, and inscribe causal stories onto the cultural psyche. Like the Harrison Act of 1914, the Marihuana Tax Act of 1937 was enforced by the U.S. Treasury Department because it was a tax law. Hence, at Treasury there was already institutional capacity, in addition to habituated practice gleaned from enforcement of Prohibition laws (repealed only four years earlier). Antinarcotics regulations remained in place and, hence, additional, similar practices were institutionally welcomed. The Bureau of Narcotics under Harry Anslinger served a gatekeeper function, fueling the usage of the emergent term *marijuana* (spelled "marihuana" in the 1930s) to displace the terms *hemp* or *cannabis*. Institutionalized practices of prohibition, which nearly ground to a halt with the repeal of the 18th amendment in 1933, were reasserting and extending themselves in a new venue; marijuana was, in effect, made illegal in 1937.

With taken-for-granted ideography and narrative on their side, status quo institutions resist challenges more successfully than when narratives compete on equal footing. For example, a documentary film produced by the Canadian Department of National Health and Welfare in 1949—that won a national film award in Canada and was praised by the United Nations Division of Narcotic Drugs— was banned in the United States at the Bureau of Narcotic's insistence because it portrayed addiction as a disease rather than a crime, because the addicts were too personable, and because the role of the police was underemphasized (Lindesmith 1965, 253). This is an example of *selecting out*. In another example, the Clinton administration in 1994 refused to release a report that needle-exchange programs reduced AIDS virus transmission without increasing drug use (Bertram et al. 1996, 123). Ideographs such as *soft on drugs* are able to crowd out *clean needles* and *harm reduction*. Indeed, the Clinton administration's 1995 National Drug Control Strategy was sharply criticized for emphasizing *hard-core users,* an ideograph that had won an established niche in the drug policy discourse. "Hard-core" users are presumably untreatable, unredeemable, and undeserving of care (Bertram et al. 1996, 124). The harm-reduction narrative challenged the view that needle-exchange programs accommodate the morally indefensible method of drug injection, but the challenge was suppressed. (In 2009, the federal prohibition was lifted [Urbina 2009].)

Status quo institutions, with a history of established habitus, relationships, and prerogatives, can influence which new ideas and practices are to be allowed into the mainstream and which are to be excluded. But where there is political will, even established institutions can be turned back. The rigidity of Prohibition, with its moral-absolutist aspirations, by its demise invites a less-rigid approach to pondering the durability of public administration's institutionalized practices, to rethink what we have traditionally referred to as institutions.

D. Defeating an Institutionalized Discourse

The advantages of status quo institutional power in framing the discourse make those instances when institutionalized power reverses itself notable. The DDT episode mentioned earlier was presented in the context of the institutionalizing of the EPA. Alcohol prohibition was reversed in the United States, to take a historically prominent example of deinstitutionalization.

The 18th Amendment, prohibiting alcohol, was ratified in 1919. By the late 1920s, Prohibition was undergoing a change in public attitude. Newspapers lamented the hypocrisy of those who were happy with Prohibition when it applied to others, especially the workingman. Editorial comment railed against the ostentatious disrespect for law that Prohibition brought. Hypocritical "dry" legislators appearing in court for possession of alcohol made delicious national news. Newspapers took exception to the imposition by force of a moral ideal of abstinence. The *New York Times* (1932) recorded a shift in sentiment from the pre-1920 era to 1932:

> The wet organization (Women's Organization for National Prohibition Reform) quoted the following campaign statements of the drys, many of them taken from the "Prohibition Ratification Handbook," "The saloons will be closed. Drinking will be reduced. Drunkenness will disappear. Crime will be reduced at least one-half. The constantly increasing cost to taxpayers in providing the saloon-made convicts, insane, imbecile and delinquent will be stopped. Liquor is a corrupter of politics." . . . Contrasting

with these statements, the organization presented the following as representing present conditions: . . . "Three speakeasies now for every saloon before prohibition. The nation's drink bill has risen over $1,000,000,000. Arrests for drunkenness are three times the number in 1920. . . . Seven million dollars was appropriated in 1929 for Federal prisons. . . . Forty million dollars a year spent by the Federal Government, $882,000,000 lost annually in Federal revenues, $100,000,000 lost annually in State revenues. Thirty-two States with a population of 100,000,000 refuse to spend one cent to enforce the law."

When alcohol prohibition was introduced, there was hope among its advocates that it would be widely supported across the nation and that everyone would recognize the harmful effects of alcohol. Instead, the consequences of Prohibition gave rise to alternative story lines.

• Prohibition had hardly put a dent in demand for alcohol.
• The terrible saloon was displaced by the even-worse speakeasy.
• Resources devoted to law enforcement increased.
• A large proportion of the population had been criminalized.
• Respect for the law diminished as people ignored it.
• Violent crime increased.
• Police corruption increased.

Prohibition had been in place for 13 years but had not achieved a perdurable presence. As Adams (1933) put it, "While its proponents have claimed that it was lifting the nation to a new plane of moral, social and economic well-being, its enemies have charged it with undermining the fundamental principles of government; breaking down respect for law and establishing an outlaw empire which, at its flood tide, extorted graft from the American people at $25,000,000 a day." The winning arguments that Prohibition was "an unwarranted attempt to regulate social habits and customs" and "an exercise of the police power which had no place in the Constitution" (Adams 1933) were voiced throughout the 1920s but finally gained ascendance during the 1932 election year. Kyvig (2000) credits the rise of single-issue pressure groups, such as the Association Against the Prohibition Amendment, the Crusaders (a volunteer lawyers' group), and the Women's Organization for National Prohibition Reform, with a major role in the turnaround. Labor unions, trade and bar associations, medical societies, and veterans' groups played supporting roles. There was pervasive disregard for the law, and the Progressive faith in social engineering that held sway in 1919 had dissipated when it was deemed an unwanted intervention in the everyday lives of citizens (Kyvig 2000).

In the case of Prohibition repeal, interest group associations energized the effort. And other kinds of associations were brought into the public conversation as well. The association of Prohibition with hypocrisy, police corruption, and unwanted government enforcement practices brought into the discourse connotations much different from Prohibition's earlier association with morality and well-being. It is to the practical power of narratives that we now turn.

III. SYMBIOTIC ASSOCIATIONS

One might suppose that in a liberal pluralist society, a dominant narrative would not necessarily need to repudiate all other narratives. A stable narrative could appreciate that there is a pluralism of realities, paradigms, and narratives operating in the same society—but that would insinuate something like a free-speech story line into every dominant narrative. Not every narrative is forgiving of heresies against it. Institutions adopt various strategies for survival. Though some narratives are willing to co-opt, or to be co-opted, institutionalized narratives are conspicuously identifiable by regularized conduct among the people who establish (and re-establish) enduring relationships through practice. These relationships between narrative and practice are symbiotic associations in that the interaction reinforces their mutual continuation.

The practical power of narratives derives from the transformation that takes place when the winning narrative is performed in practice. Ideographs and narratives are interpreted and made meaningful in context; they are enacted and performed even as they are being expressed. The symbiosis of expression and performance entails a network of associations common to both, collapsing the dichotomy expression versus execution.

Action, value commitments, and relationships are simultaneously expressed and executed in the performance by the actors (and objects) involved in the process. The physical context is necessarily part of the symbiotic associations entailed in the performance of practice. Schön and Rein (1994, 169) brought objects into the picture because policy actors have "conversations with materials." Such conversations are entailed in the performance policy-related activity. To illustrate how associations are performed, it helps to distinguish between the concept *ostensive,* which refers to the stuff that remains there, whatever happens to the onlooker, and the concept of *performative,* which vanishes when it is no longer performed (Latour 2005). As Latour (2005, 34) put it, "Social aggregates are not the object of an *ostensive* definition—like mugs and cats and chairs that can be pointed at by the index finger—but only of a *performative* definition. They are made by the various ways and manners in which they are said to exist." These performances have the effect of creating social aggregates. A social aggregate can become an organization, created by the associations and performances that constitute organizational action. Organizational structure is often taken to be an ostensive object, rather than a social aggregate that has to be performed. To stop making and remaking social collectivities, such as administrative organizations, is to do away with social collectivities, such as administrative organizations. Not fixity, but performative activity supports constant regrouping. What appear to be social structures ("are said to exist" in Latour's terminology) are instead performed regularities. Performances are the specific actions taken by organizational members in concert with others and with other objects. (An office environment might include, for example, ostensive objects such as computers, forms, databases, or whatever tools and objects are relevant to the situation.) The upshot here is that organizations are not causal independent variables; they are shorthand markers we use in conversations; they are said to exist. But the performance of the ritual, of the network of associations, is the life of an organization.

Routine actions sometimes can be taken almost effortlessly, but there is always an element of improvisation involved because the action could always be performed in a slightly different manner. Self-monitoring, reinterpretation (of the rules, the situation, the usefulness of various tools, the work setting, or the meaning of the action), or even slipups can influence the action for better or worse. Resistance to and enforcement of power relations within the social setting are additional modifying effects on the fidelity to the ritual. In addition, others' actions may be taken into account, and, indeed, must be when organized, collective performance is undertaken. The opportunities for variation and exceptions are extensive; it would be an error to simply assume the presence of a stable structure without acknowledging that social order, as well as social change, requires performance.

The regularity and customs on which entrenched practices rely for their entrenchment are learned not by reading the organizational manuals and rule books carefully but by reproducing accurately the network of associations relevant to the situation. And according to Bourdieu (1977, 18), "If agents are possessed by their habitus more than they possess it, this is because it acts within them as the organizing principle of their actions, and because this *modus operandi* informing all thought and action (including thought of action) reveals itself only in the *opus operatum*." In other words, habitus uses networks of durable dispositions to perform certain rites, visible in their effects if not in their performance. A collective task relies on habitus to generate regularized practices. The habitus gets its gusto from the continuous reinforcement of symbiotic associations that each participant receives/expresses; habitus requires little in the way of intentionality, but it does require performance. To find out what is going on in public management, one must investigate the networks of association, including meaning associations, at the level of practice. Latour (2005) thinks this can be done. His aim would be to describe and account for displacements, for changes to understandings, for alterations in practices. Successful research must find an acceptable and effective way of discovering what each participant, actor, and object in the institution thinks it is doing. However, if the habitus is anything like a collective unconscious, the answers to the "what do you think you are doing?" question may be hard to come by. In the narrative approach, people and objects do not necessarily know why they are doing something.

If old practices ritualize old narratives, emergent practices bring multiple new associations into the interactive mix; hence, something new is performed—through new associations more so than telos.

Symbiotic association among practices, narratives, and objects can defeat oppressive structures because structures are themselves nothing but the performance of symbiotic association. Meaning is modified when old registrations on the list of associations are displaced and new registrations are enrolled in the network. Change happens when associations are gathered together into new shapes. Elements of the network might now be interpreted differently and enacted differently. Human interactions are opportunities for associations among ideographs, objects, facts, and practices to form and express themselves. Such associations are distributed throughout the institutional habitus and can come in from outside it—both exogenous and endogenous associations are allowed (unless prohibited by management, which may believe that limiting associations is necessary to maintain a particular task orientation—more on this in the next section). All the ideographs, objects, facts, and practices of the network have a history, which is more or less difficult to trace. They may or may not have originated in the dominant narrative implemented at the genesis. Yet, in association together, a symbiosis of such ingredients produces effects when performed.

Situational associations typically include the practices of one's specialization and training, the cultural cues brought into the situation from outside the dominant policy narrative, and the standardized rules forced into practice by the local authority. The regularity and coherence of policy implementation and its administration does not require a rational basis; accident and contingency can also join a network and produce effects. Networks of symbiotic association have the capability to transform practices. They function as a matrix of perceptions, appreciations, and actions; they make possible infinitely diversified tasks. They can stimulate others, demanding some kind of response from those who are disposed to the same habitus. And yet, no tie is as durable or as static as the current social order (the institutionalized habitus) makes it seem to be.

Openness to new ideas, new associations, new relationships, and new disasters may threaten managerial control, but such openness may serve well the demands on public policy and administration going into the future.

IV. A QUINTESSENTIAL 21ST-CENTURY POLICY PROBLEM

One constellation of meanings and objects that provides an illustration of how associations might play out is the StarLink episode, which Kettl (2001, 3) describes as "the quintessential twenty-first century policy problem." StarLink was a patented brand of transgenic maize—corn that has been genetically modified to immunize the plant against a parasitic corn borer. An elementary map of the complex of associations entailed in the problem gives us a glimpse of how a public policy/administration problem might appear as a dynamic moment in a constellation of meanings and objects:

- Corn borer → damaged corn → loss of grain → loss of millions of dollars
- Aventis Crop Sciences (large biotechnology company) → discovered a way to implant a bacteria gene into corn → new breed of corn → successfully impeded corn borer → reduced loss of grain → recovered the loss of millions of dollars
- However: new breed of corn → StarLink → contains protein $C_{ry9}C$; $C_{ry9}C$ → allergies in some people; → approved as animal feed but with EPA-mandated 660-foot buffer zone around cornfields
- StarLink → found in human food → entered media hyperreality → shut down of cornflakes lines
- Causal story → disrespect of buffer zone, careless planting → wind → cross-contamination with human-use corn
- Japan, largest importer of U.S. agricultural products → found traces of Star-Link in shipments; recipient countries in Africa → refused to accept aid because of StarLink
- Negative image of StarLink → corporate refusals to purchase bioengineered crops → governmental proposals to require more labeling and information of content of food items → Aventis asked EPA to cancel its registration, withdrawing product from market

Responsibility for solving the problem was difficult to pinpoint. The EPA was involved, and so were the U.S. Department of Agriculture, the Food and Drug Administration, the Centers for Disease Control, and even the United Nations. Several private corporations were also involved, as was the Japanese government. Practices of split approval (OK for animals but not OK for humans) were called into question. The upshot for public policy and administration is that effective and agile agencies of governing might organize themselves according to the ever-changing and quickly evolving networks of symbiotic associations that swirl around public policy problems. No longer are willful, intentional humans the only performers in the picture; wind blowing across the buffer zone, proteins, allergies, genes, and cornfields claim their share of transformative power. As these associations played out, new ideography such as *Frankenfood* entered the political discourse.

The underlying driver of social order is not some innate stasis or fixed structure, but the performance of practices reinforced through interaction and association. The implication of this shift of thinking is to refocus attention from stasis to associative performance. Association—including ideographic connotations, associations with objects, associations with practices, and associations with people—accounts for the performance. By thinking of association this way, the fragility of the social order is kept alive and its permanence is no longer taken for granted. Ideas, images, and ideographs flow through the associative network, connecting things that may not even be social or even human, and sometimes transforming them. Associations make institutions come into being or endure or decay or disappear. Old associations can mutate into new or different ones. Yet, there is no reservoir of associative ties in the ostensive sense; an association must be performed.

Objects, facts, and practices as well as ideographic, linguistic, and symbolic stuff comprise the social interactions of the habitus, which resemble the networks of association that Latour (2005, 66) described: "If action is limited a priori to what 'intentional,' 'meaningful' humans do, it is hard to see how a hammer, a basket, a door closer, a cat, a rug, a mug, a list, or a tag could act. They might exist in the domain of 'material' 'causal' relations, but not the 'reflexive' 'symbolic' domain of social relations. By contrast, if we stick to our decision to start from the controversies . . . then *any thing* that does modify a state of affairs by making a difference is an actor." To grasp this point, imagine driving a nail into wood without a hammer; and then consider including the hammer among the symbiotic associations that comprise actions. The hammer and the nail, along with mental focus, physical skill, and hand-eye coordination are part of the performance. Performance describes the things and ideas and techniques and objects—the assemblage of associations—that inform social action. Narrative performance thus binds ideas to action.

6
Conclusion

The idea of mobilizing symbols that shape policy narratives begins to take shape with the connotative associations inherent in the term *ideography*. Ideography, in turn, directs attention to semantic associations, to similarities and differences in symbolic meanings, to emotional resonance, to value orientation. Ideographs pull together multiple signs, references, and images to signify an understanding that is imbued with cognition, emotional resonance, situational awareness, and values. These are the relevant elements of public policy discourse; these elements are expansive, sometimes beyond the bounds of reason.

Public policy discourse expresses ideographic images quite regularly: acid rain, drug lord, flood of immigrants, partial birth abortion, no child left behind, and, ironically enough, objective fact are examples of such imagery. The connotative depth and range of these ideographs vary, but all are easily exploitable in the art of meaning capture. Evidence, data, research, reasoned argument—all are valuable aims of rational inquiry, but public policy discourse does not typically work like scholarly argumentation. Causality functions differently in policy discourse than it does in scientific research. Causality is frequently part of a narrative that frames the issue by assessing blame for problem, warranting a solution, or justifying inaction.

Epistemologically, the narrative approach is necessarily interpretive. One can count the number of times the term *drug addict* shows up in a sample of publications, but it is a matter of interpretation to discern whether the ideograph is a criminal type of drug addict or merely a diseased drug addict from the harm-reduction narrative. Indeed, facts themselves are social constructions (Poovey 1998); some are well crafted and some are poorly crafted (Latour 2005). The relationship between indicators and facts is forever problematic because languages are self-referential epiphenomena. In semiotics, words do not refer to objects but rather to mental pictures of those objects, making language highly transportable in that one can talk about objects that are not physically present. But there is a gap between the word that would serve as indicator and "reality itself." In the social sciences, this gap is highly problematic. We live in a material, prelinguistic natural world that the narrative approach accepts, but, once we begin to discuss policy problems with one another, we are at the mercy of a particular language. Even signs that effectively denote some aspect of the objective world can be used again to connote something else. Blue sky can mean more than a sky that is blue. There are good scientific reasons for trying to denotatively attach a signifier to a specific object, but the poets (and paid hacks) of policy discourse will always find another connotation or a new association.

The absence of foundational fixity does not rob society of meaning; to the contrary, malleability enables meaning to develop, grow, and change. Meaning making is an omnipresent communicative social activity. Narratives and their ideography are connotative and holistic, important not for their denotative precision so much as their integration of meaning into a form of coherence. Meanings can be changed, through new or altered associations among signs, ideographs, and narratives. When meanings change, the symbiotic relations between narrative and practice changes the way tasks are accomplished or understood. The legitimacy and appropriateness of social practices change when meanings change.

To maximize stability and order, one might prefer as little change as possible. Managerial control can be thought of as techniques and tactics for limiting or somehow disciplining the actionable associations that emerge in an organization or that infiltrate from outside. However, an overemphasis on this sort of managerial discipline obviates creative experimentation with new associations, impeding adaptation to turbulent environments and diminishing the opportunities for creative solutions to complex problems. Diamond (2005) described occasions when societies have collapsed. These collapses were due in part to ecological problems but were also due to social practices that were incompatible with sustaining the local natural environment. Inflexibility in changing practices and their symbiotic narratives can prove ruinous. For a practicing public administrator it is equally valid to worry about too much institutionalized control (that might snuff out alternatives) as too little institutional stability and integration (that might lead to chaos and loss of efficacy). The habitual conventions of institutionalized practice enable coordination and fulfillment of mutual expectations. A narrative thus entrenched into institutionalized practice is able to reject alternative practices that would implement some competing narrative. It is possible that narrative inflexibility could threaten discursive democracy. In contexts of discursive democracy, there is freedom to make new associations and connotations, to experiment with and legitimate new actions and social practices; upstart heretical narratives are allowed to compete against a dominant status quo narrative.

Changes to an agency's practices take place in the context of political and social narratives that articulate new combinations of values, facts, skills, objects, and ideography. Changing practices entails politics because historically built-up narratives provide a commonsense understanding that warrants current practice and the status quo. The narrative approach takes politics to mean the attempt to displace one idea with another, one ideograph with another, one practice with another at a moment of impasse. Impasses can appear in culture-wide debates about the role of government or at the micro level of work tasks. This moment of potential change calls into question the historical status quo. When social practices change, meanings and associations have also changed. However, it would be a mistake to equate change with action. The status quo is not the absence of action and performance. Regularized social action and habitual practice must be performed anew each day. Cultural habits and social practices must be enacted and accurately reenacted to produce the stability they are credited with. Habitus, produced in a sphere of commonality, normalizes and naturalizes ways of doing and thinking (even though these ways could have been otherwise and may yet be). Existing customs and practices are reproduced (replicated) accurately through their associations, as the habitus expresses them. Symbiotic associations—of objects, practices, and ideas—need to be performed if there is to be either change *or* stability.

The performance of associations—the networks of dispositions to perform certain rites—is not necessarily visible, but the effects are. The effects may look like organizational structure to some or policy implementation or public administration or accomplishment of some collective task. The associations, if we could see them, may include the values of the agency's original policy narrative, a sampling of the latest managerial fads, second-nature habits of mind, cultural norms from the environment, local techniques and concepts, tactics of governmental rationality, and so on. It would therefore be misleading to think of institutionalized practices as "structure." The term *structure* encourages researchers to leave performance unexamined. Thinking in terms of "structure" takes for granted the accurate performance of the rituals and customs. Instead, thinking in terms of symbiotic associations among narratives, practices, relations, and objects in the environment brings the focus on performance of stabilizing rituals.

The stabilizing rituals of policy implementation/management/administration must be performed in practice and so, too, must policy change. At political moments—moments of impasse—policy narratives can move history.

Appendix 1
Narratives in Drug Policy

The purpose of this appendix, which contains illustrative case examples of drug policy discourse from multiple perspectives, is to help demonstrate the importance of narrative in public policy discourse by showing the different ways that different perspectives, with their different interpretations and different facts, are brought to bear on drug policy. The connotative powers of signs, ideographs, and narratives are illustrated primarily with examples from the war on drugs. Attitudes toward, say, a drug addict, are shaped by the ideographic images attached to the term. Drug addict could mean "criminal to be imprisoned" or it could mean "diseased person in need of treatment." Each narrative has its own distinguishing facts, logic, ideography, and objective evidence.

I. NARRATIVE AS PERSPECTIVE

In drug policy, the institutionalized narrative—the one that has found its way into practice—understands drug addicts as criminals worthy of incarceration, drugs as something to be prohibited from use, production of these drugs as something to be eradicated, and supply of them as something to be interdicted. Ideography and narrative coherence—not rational coherence—secure the legitimacy of the resulting social practices (incarceration of repeat offenders, for example) and further function to fend off competing narratives. Competing, nondominant narratives frame drug addiction as a public health problem or drug use as a matter of consumer choice, but in the American context these have been losing narratives.

The major fault line in drug policy discourse forms around the question of criminalization. Hence, this appendix will organize itself around narratives that 1) imply that those who use drugs are to be classified as criminals, and 2) narratives that do not.

II. NARRATIVES IMPLYING CRIMINALITY

In this section, aspects of the winning narratives are presented. The abstinence narrative and nativism have powerfully informed drug policy in the United States by providing ideographic coherence to policies that now have considerable institutional history.

A. Abstinence

America of the 19th century could be called a dope fiend's paradise (Brecher 1972). Opiates and many other drugs were readily available. Brecher (3) lists several legal channels of distribution, including:

• physicians dispensing opiates directly to patients or writing prescriptions
• drugstores and pharmacies selling opiates over the counter
• grocery stores and general stores selling opiates
• opiates ordered by mail
• patent medicines purchased, many of which contain narcotics

None of this was seen as a problem through most of the 19th century. Physicians began to notice habitual drug use among former soldiers, who had been wounded in the Civil War and were given morphine for pain. Years later, many of these veterans were continuing to use the drug. Drug habitués in the general population, too, were becoming more conspicuous in the latter part of the century. By 1903 the American Pharmaceutical Association was urging that cocaine and opium derivatives be disbursed only with a prescription and that drug use should be regulated. When the reformers of the Progressive era joined forces with doctors and pharmacists on this recommendation, regulation of narcotics commenced. Once the Pure Food and Drug Act of 1906 was enacted, narcotic ingredients had to be listed on products that crossed state lines (Bertram et al. 1996, 63).

The avowed purpose of antinarcotic activism was prevention of addiction at first but evolved into a broader movement against drinking, gambling, and prostitution (Bertram et al. 1996, 63). The American Temperance Society, founded in 1826, required its members to refrain from drinking distilled beverages, though consuming fermented beverages, such as beer and wine, was apparently tolerated. As the preacher Lyman Beecher put it in 1826, "Intemperance is a national sin. . . . It is in vain to rely alone upon self-government, and voluntary abstinence. . . . The remedy, whatever it may be, must be universal, operating permanently, at all times, and in all places. . . . It is the banishment of ardent spirits from the list of lawful articles of commerce" (Beecher 2002, 68–69). The idea of temperance soon transformed into an idea of total abstinence. As Musto (2002, 9) described the progression, "Beecher's argument that total abstinence is the inevitable final stage of temperance gradually achieved dominance. In 1836 the American Temperance Society . . . officially changed its definition of temperance to abstinence." The move from temperance to abstinence moves the narrative one step closer to criminalization; alcohol would be criminalized in 1919.

The Women's Christian Temperance Union (WCTU), concerned about the connection between alcohol and domestic violence and other family and social problems, declared the consumption of alcohol to be un-Christian. Drinking for pleasure is dangerous and unnecessary. In defending home and family, women found an entrée into American political life. In the cultural ideography of the late 1800s, women were particularly well positioned to express moral purity and virtue (Stivers 1993, 79–80).

Abstinence went hand in hand with prevention when it came to the use of dangerous drugs. A young woman writing anonymously to her doctor in 1889 described her miserable regrets of going through opium withdrawal, the burden she imposed on her mother with her indifference, laziness, and lack of remedy and concluded with some finger-pointing: "You doctors know all the harm those drugs do, as well as the 'victims' of them, and yet you do precious little to prevent it" (Anonymous 2002, 228). The call to action was slowly but surely heeded over the next century. The prevention that Ms. Anonymous urged would eventually take the form of abstinence, prohibition, and absolutism.

Absolutism, whose ideography is most evident in alcohol prohibition narratives but evident in opium prohibition as well, found its way into public policy in the 1980s, as evidenced by the warnings that continue to appear on contemporary American beer labels: "According to the surgeon general, women should not drink alcoholic beverages during pregnancy because of the risk of birth defects." In their oversight role regarding prevention messages, the policy makers at the U.S. Department of Health and Human Services rejected a safe upper limit of consumption of alcohol. They found recommendations regarding *des-*

ignated drivers to be unacceptable because that would imply that drinking to the point of intoxication is fine so long as one does not then drive (Musto 2002, 5). Regarding drinking while pregnant, Department of Health and Human Services' guidelines state, "Since not enough is known about how much alcohol is acceptable, for whom, and during which stages of pregnancy, the safest choice is not to drink during pregnancy" (cited in Musto 2002, 6). There had been no link established between alcohol and harm to the fetus until 1970 when a pediatrics resident at the University of Washington found what she thought were similarities in the facial appearances of babies born to welfare mothers who were heavy drinkers. Research into this possibility soon generated a new disease: fetal alcohol syndrome. In 1977, the federal government stated, "While safe levels of drinking are unknown, it appears that a risk is established with ingestion above 3 ounces of absolute alcohol or 6 drinks per day. Between 1 ounce and 3 ounces, there is still uncertainty but caution is advised" (cited in Musto 2002, 170). Such nuance was lost by the last year of the Reagan administration. To prevent fetal alcohol syndrome, the Anti-Drug Abuse Act of 1988 required all alcoholic beverage containers to issue warning labels telling women they should not drink alcoholic beverages during pregnancy (Musto 2002, 172; in chapter 24 Musto presents the exact language of the act). Temperance, in the cause of prevention, yielded again to absolute abstention—this time for pregnant women, even though no medical evidence indicates that an ounce of alcohol per day produced any health risks for mother or child. As Musto (2002, 12) put it, "In America, prohibition had an appeal as the final and necessary statement of disapproval."

Prohibitionist concerns about drugs and alcohol are often justified by the negative conditions with which they are associated. According to Tonry (1990, 1), "Drug abuse and drug trafficking are inextricably related to the deterioration of many inner-cities, to heightened levels of violence within the drug markets, and to a variety of social and personal pathologies." Nearly 20 million Americans aged 12 or over—8 percent of the population—have used illegal drugs in the past month, according to the 2007 National Survey on Drug Use and Health (Department of Health and Human Services 2008). According to Falco (1992, 9), citing the National Academy of Sciences, 5.5 million Americans have drug problems sufficiently severe to require treatment. News accounts have documented this cause for alarm: crack-addicted mothers, having passed their addictions on to their offspring, proceed to neglect them. *Time* magazine's May 13, 1991, cover had a picture of a crying child with the lead story titled "Crack Kids: Their Mothers Used Drugs, and Now It's the Children Who Suffer." When these children are older, as the story prophesizes, they will, in due course, become runners and lookouts for drug-dealing gangs. James (1998, 1) presents a vivid image in an antidrug pamphlet: "Police found him in a closet, with both legs—and eight other bones—broken. Covered with bruises, he was hiding from the monsters who hurt him—his crack-addicted parents." Meanwhile, innocent bystanders—especially poor people who live in the same neighborhoods—are victims of shoot-outs among rival gangs. In this story line, cocaine and crack dealing offer potentially profitable business opportunities for young entrepreneurs, curtailing their willingness to work at minimum-wage, legally sanctioned jobs. According to Pres. Ronald Reagan, "Drug abuse is a repudiation of everything America is. The destructiveness and human wreckage mock our heritage" (Bertram et al. 1996, 139).

While it is difficult to calculate the social costs of illegal drugs because of the weakness of drug abuse indicators, the National Institute on Drug Abuse and National Institute on Alcohol Abuse and Alcoholism (1992) once estimated the cost to be $110 billion each year, taking into account accidents, crime, domestic violence, illness, lost opportunity, and reduced productivity. The National Drug Control Strategy (2009) emphasizes expanding treatment capacity and creating effective workplace programs and prevention policies, while continuing to target drug supply, trafficking, and money laundering as official U.S. policy. The document further claims that drug users' absenteeism, accidents and injuries, low morale, and serious productivity losses are among the costs of drug abuse. Though relating drug abuse to loss of worker productivity makes intuitive sense, Duncan (2002) could not find any study that directly measured the impact of drug abuse on worker productivity. Most studies used proxy measures that typically correlated drug dependence (rather than drug use) with productivity effects. Moreover, he found, alcohol abuse seems to have a much stronger relationship to lost productivity than does illegal drug abuse. Duncan also noted that urine testing is unlikely to improve workplace productivity because urine screening cannot distinguish between a user and an abuser or someone who uses on the job and someone who does not. In their regression analysis, Shepard and Clifton (1998) found that drug testing correlated with *lowered* productivity.

Challenges such as Duncan's and Shepard and Clifton's seem beside the point that Franklin Roosevelt (2002, 151) long ago acknowledged in reference to alcohol: "It is increasingly apparent that the intemperate use of intoxicants has no place in this new mechanized civilization of ours. In our industry, in our recreation, on our highways, a drunken man is more than an objectionable companion; he is a peril to the rest of us. The hand that controls the machinery of our factories, that holds the steering wheel of our automobiles, and the brains that guide the course of finance and industry, should alike be free from the effects of over-indulgence in alcohol."

When the abstinence narrative enters policy discourse, however, the policy upshot is usually, but not always, that drugs should be absolutely prohibited. Alcoholics Anonymous (AA) famously shies away from entering policy discourse or making society-wide proclamations about how those outside the AA context should conduct themselves, yet, their purpose is indeed alcohol abstinence, achieved one day at a time (Kurtz 1979). In the abstinence-policy narrative, drugs (precisely which one is only sometimes specified) are a form of pollution, a contaminant not only of the physical body but also of the spirit and social fabric of the community. The temptation of inebriants is something to resist, absolutely. For the virtuous abstinent, the appropriate public policy is, typically, to launch and sustain a zero-tolerance policy that will decrease the import of illegal drugs, the domestic sale of them, and the personal use of these same harmful drugs. Adolescents in particular should just say "no" to drugs.

From a nativist perspective, the policy implications are similar, but the images and story lines brought into the narrative are quite different, as we shall see.

B. Nativism

The nativist narrative presents a picture of drug users as betrayers of patriotism and American values. Drug users are a threat to decent society. The term *nativism* was used by Kinder (1992) to refer to a tendency to associate drug use with minorities, exemplified by Harry Anslinger's rhetoric in the 1930s as head of the Federal Bureau of Narcotics. The nativist narrative marginalizes drug users and would exclude them from normal society by casting them as *the other,* which is to say an ethnic or racial minority or some group that exemplifies *not-us.*

The moments in American history when one drug or another first became illegal are telling. Chinese people were drawn to the California Gold Rush after the Civil War, but by 1882 Chinese immigration was halted by federal law. This change took place amidst some rather severe anti-Chinese public discourse, which reached a high-pitched low point in the 1870s. Chinese workers were blamed for downward wage pressures in the labor market, and they became targets of bigotry and prejudice. Helmer (1975, 31) located a California Senate report from 1877 stating, "The whites cannot stand their dirt and the fumes of opium." In 1875, San Francisco outlawed the smoking of opium—the first time drugs had been banned in the United States. Curiously, only the *smoking* of opium and morphine was banned. Chinese immigrants smoked opium; ingestion of opium by means other than smoking it remained legal (Meier 1994, 23). The association of opium smoking with Chinese immigration "was one of the earliest examples of a powerful theme in the American perception of drugs, that is, linkage between a drug and a feared or rejected group within our society. Cocaine and marijuana would be similarly linked" (Musto 2002, 184–185).

Drug policy removes "a superfluous pool of already marginalized segments of the black population" (Bertram et al. 1996, 43). In order to get southern Demo-

pass the Marihuana Tax Act in 1937. *Reefer Madness,* a film produced in 1936, attempted to associate marijuana smoking with manslaughter, rape, suicide, and madness (http://video.google.com/videoplay?docid=-6696582420128930236).

Anslinger's writing style was more spectacular than the movie. "The sprawled body of a young girl lay crushed on the sidewalk the other day after a plunge from the fifth story of a Chicago apartment house. Everyone called it suicide, but actually it was murder. The killer was a narcotic known to America as marihuana. . . . How many murders, suicides, robberies, criminal assaults, holdups, burglaries, and deeds of maniacal insanity it causes each year, especially among the young, can be only conjectured" (Anslinger and Cooper 2002, 433). Anslinger and Cooper further speculate that the marijuana cigarettes "may have been sold by a hot tamale vendor" (434). They also claimed in the same essay that after smoking marijuana, a young man in Florida was found "staggering about in a human slaughterhouse. With an ax he had killed his father, his mother, two brothers, and a sister" (435). Some of the prose was published in official documents of Anslinger's Federal Bureau of Narcotics. Anslinger made a point of quoting judges who shared his writing style. One judge allegedly said, "I consider marihuana the worst of all narcotics—far worse than the use of morphine or cocaine. Under its influence men have become beasts. . . . Marihuana destroys life itself" (cited in Musto 2002, 429).

The vivid imagery and reckless associations asserted by Anslinger and other antidrug warriors have helped shape the debate that resulted in enactment and implementation of antidrug policy. Once implemented, the continuation of antidrug practices persists through inertia, although commentators often describe the institutionalization of enforcement practices in conspiratorial terms. In the next section, we turn to the narratives whose policy implication is that drug use should be decriminalized, as least to some extent and possibly completely. These are the fairness narrative, the harm-avoidance narrative, the libertarian narrative, and the futility narrative.

III. NARRATIVES THAT DO NOT IMPLY CRIMINALITY

Cigarette smoking, which was once as American as the Marlboro man, is increasingly eschewed because of its serious health effects. The definition of *normal* has changed over time. The image of drug users changes over time. The categories of targeted people change over time. The more tolerant the culture, the more groups can be different without being stigmatized. But the criteria for determining which inebriant/stimulant is punishable and which is acceptable are so frivolously arbitrary that this system of otherizing functions against any notion of justice. There is the problem of fairness.

A. Fairness

Standards for criminality and sentencing seem irrational. Cannabis smoking is less risky than either cigarette smoking or alcohol, yet, those two are legal. The badness of the drug has no rational relationship with how the legal system categorizes them. Marijuana is classified as a felony narcotic, even though medical cannabis may be useful in treating a wide variety of diseases and conditions (Herer 2000). Nonetheless, in the United States there were 481,098 marijuana arrests in 1994 (Thomas 1996), which increased to 872,721 by 2007 (Belville 2008). In 1994, 83.7 percent of these were for possession and not sale or manufacture. This percentage increased to 89 percent in 2007. Between 2007 and 2010 marijuana arrests declined from 872,720 to 858,408 (http://www.drugwarfacts .org/cms/Marijuana#TotalUniform Crime Report, citing FBI Uniform Crime Report 2010).

In the fairness narrative, the legal status of a drug is not related to the harm (or benefit) caused by the substance. Estimated per capita death rates for different drugs are presented in table 1. Ostrowski (1990, 53) is distinguishing between those who died from *enforcement* and those who have died from *use* (as with an overdose). For heroin and cocaine, the figures in parentheses include collateral deaths due to enforcement as well as deaths due to use. Marijuana is not included in the chart because there are no confirmed deaths traceable to marijuana *use*.

As Ostrowski (1990, 53) summarized, "Thus, for every death caused by the intrinsic effects of cocaine, heroin kills 20, alcohol kills 37 and tobacco kills 132." The legality of a drug is unrelated to the harm (or benefit) caused except through law enforcement. And the punishment for possession of the drug is equally arbitrary.

Consider too the findings of Nutt et al. (2007). This study asked two groups

Table 1. Death rates for selected drugs

Drug	Users	Deaths per year	Deaths per 100,000 users
Tobacco	60 million	390,000	650
Alcohol	100 million	150,000	150
Heroin	500,000	400	80 (400)*
Cocaine	5 million	200	4 (20)*

Source: Ostrowski 1990, 53

* Figures in parentheses include collateral deaths due to enforcement as well as deaths due to use.

of experts to rank drugs using three criteria: 1) physical harm to user; 2) potential for addiction; 3) impact on society. One group was on the registry of specialists in addiction at the Royal College of Psychiatrists in the United Kingdom. The second group included experts in diverse disciplines. Respondents were given the opportunity to revise their rankings in light of discussions, which took place over four meetings because the number of drugs being considered was large (20). The ranking (physical harm + potential for addiction + impact on society) was as follows:

1. heroin
2. cocaine
3. barbiturates
4. street methadone
5. alcohol
6. ketamine
7. benzodiazepines
8. amphetamine
9. tobacco
10. buprenorphine
11. marijuana
12. solvents
13. 4-MTA
14. LSD
15. methylphenidate
16. anabolic steroids
17. GHB
18. ecstasy
19. alkyl nitrates
20. khat

A different comparison of addictive properties of popular drugs appeared in the *New York Times,* which attributed the ranking criteria to Dr. Jack E. Henningfield of the National Institute on Drug Abuse and Dr. Neal L. Benowitz of the University of California at San Francisco (Hilts 1994). Common Sense for Drug Policy utilized Henningfield's ratings in chart 1.

The six drugs were compared and ranked from one to six, according to five criteria:

Dependence measures how difficult it is for the user to quit, the relapse rate, the percentage of people who eventually become dependent, the rating users give

Chart 1. How experts rate problem substances

Comparing Dangers of Popular Drugs
(Lower score indicates less serious effect)

	Nicotine	Heroin	Cocaine	Alcohol	Caffeine	Marijuana
DEPENDENCE	6	5	4	3	2	1
WITHDRAWAL	4	5	3	6	2	1
TOLERANCE	5	6	3	4	2	1
REINFORCEMENT	3	5	6	4	1	2
INTOXICATION	2	5	4	6	1	3

Source: Common Sense for Drug Policy (http://www.drugwarfacts.org/cms/node/3, accessed Dec. 2, 2011)

their own need for the substance, and the degree to which the substance will be used in the face of evidence that it causes harm.

Withdrawal considers the presence and severity of characteristic withdrawal symptoms.

Tolerance takes into account how much of the substance is needed to satisfy increasing cravings for it and the level of stable need that is eventually reached.

Reinforcement measures the substance's ability, in human and animal tests, to get users to take it again and again, and in preference to other substances.

Intoxication, though not usually counted as a measure of addiction in itself, considers the level of intoxication that is associated with addiction, and the increase in the personal and social damage a substance may do.

These sorts of comparative studies may or may not be valid, but they assuredly cast doubt on the criminal classification system of drugs. Which drugs are legal and which are illegal is not based on rational criteria. Variability in prison sentences for using or selling these substances is detached from the severity of the drug's harm as measured by risk to self and society. Despite its addictive qualities, alcohol is allowed to be advertised on television even when minors are likely to be watching. Meier (1994, 252) described the irrationality this way: "Nicotine, a highly dangerous and toxic drug, is legal and so lightly regulated that it is accessible to virtually everyone. Alcohol, a drug linked to serious health consequences, is legal but regulated with some degree of vigor. . . . Cocaine, heroin, and a variety of narcotics . . . are illegal, and the laws are aggressively enforced. . . . When viewed in their entirety, U.S. drug control policies are simply irrational."

Racial disparities are also a fairness issue. Human Rights Watch (2009) ana-lyzed arrest data they obtained from the FBI and found that blacks are dispro-portionally arrested on drug charges relative to the population at large, some years less than 3 times the rate and some years more than 5 times the usual rate. In some states, the rate was 11 times more likely. Human Rights Watch (2009, 1) further reported, "The higher rates of black drug arrests do not reflect higher rates of black drug offending. . . . [B]lacks and whites engage in drug offenses—possession and sales—at roughly comparable rates. But because black drug of-fenders are the principal targets in the 'war on drugs,' the burden of drug arrests and incarceration falls disproportionately on black men and women, their fami-lies and neighborhoods. The human as well as social, economic and political toll is as incalculable as it is unjust." The report also notes that, from 1999 through 2007, 80 percent of all drug arrests were for possession as opposed to dealing.

The fairness narrative uses discrepancies and critical logic to assess the fair-ness of drug policy and finds current policy wanting. The harm-avoidance nar-rative also interjects rationality into the debate but with a specific normative aspiration—to reduce harm.

B. Harm Avoidance

Under the banner "harm avoidance," a drug reform movement is attempting to introduce some rationality into the drug policy debate. Drug use is regarded as a health problem that is not necessarily solved by incarcerating people, which usually does more harm than good. While affirming that drug abuse is a social problem in need of attention, the policy upshot of the "harm-avoidance" nar-rative would be to offer some kind of health care therapy to victims of drug ad-diction and drug abuse.

This was the intent of California's 1961 civil commitment program in which supposed addicts were sentenced to treatment rather than imprisoned (Bertram et al. 1996, 92), as well as Proposition 36 (also known as the Substance Abuse and Crime Prevention Act of 2000), which allowed nonviolent users or possessors of illegal drugs to receive treatment rather than incarceration (Reynolds 2009). In the first year of the Proposition 36 program, over 30,000 drug offenders had been referred to certified outpatient programs, increasing their caseload by 81 percent (Reynolds 2009, 52). In California a "Harm Reduction Coalition" focuses on HIV, syringe access, drug treatment, and safer use of drugs. This coalition seeks to promote the health and dignity of those impacted by drug use.

In 1977, Pres. Jimmy Carter wrote, "My goals are to discourage all drug abuse in America—and also discourage the excessive use of alcohol and tobacco—and to reduce to a minimum the harm drug abuse causes when it does occur. . . . Marijuana continues to be an emotional and controversial issue. After four decades, efforts to discourage its use with stringent laws have still not been successful. . . . I support legislation amending Federal law to eliminate all Federal criminal penalties for the possession of up to one ounce of marijuana" (cited in Woolley and Peters, n.d.). The harm-avoidance narrative discourages the use of marijuana but without defining the smoker as a criminal. Addiction takes place in a social context involving family and friends—who often experience harm. Harm can also extend to the workplace. If smoking heroin causes less harm than injecting it (for example, spreading the AIDS virus by sharing needles), then addicts should be encouraged to smoke it or should be given clean needles.

Stanley Yolles from the National Institute of Mental Health told the House Select Committee on Crime in 1969 that drug abuse is an illness and that prison sentences are irrationally long, some up to 20 years. "Even murderers with life sentences can come up for parole after about seven years" (cited in Brecher 1972, 57). Moreover, Yolles testified, from a mental health perspective, prison experience is psychologically shattering for the young people who are incarcerated and may destroy the prospects of rehabilitation. Rep. Albert Watson of South Carolina responded: "Dr. Yolles's views are an affront to every decent law-abiding citizen in America. At a time when we are on the verge of a narcotics crisis, a supposedly responsible Federal official comes along with the incredibly ridiculous idea of dropping mandatory jail sentences for those who push dope" (cited in Brecher 1972, 57). Watson then called on Yolles to resign his position.

A Latin American commission, led by former presidents of Brazil, Mexico, and Colombia, decried the violence and corruption associated with the illegality of narcotics, the power that criminalization gives to the drug cartels, as well as the fact that interdiction and criminalization have not worked (Huffington 2009). The former presidents called for a change in the description of "addicts" to "patients," who should be taken care of in a public health system.

In the harm-reduction narrative, drug policies across the board should be changed. As Brecher (1972, 528) put it, "The one overwhelming objection to opium, morphine, heroin, and the other narcotics is the fact that they are addicting. The other disastrous effects of narcotics addiction on mind, body, and society are primarily the results of laws and policies." It would cause less harm to allow heroin addicts to enroll in methadone-maintenance programs because "it frees addicts from the heroin [demon], which is ruining their lives, and it is therefore capable of turning a majority of heroin addicts into law-abiding citizens (like pre-1914 addicts)" (529).

Another attempt to back away from the criminalization of drugs comes from the libertarian quarter.

C. Libertarian

The economist Milton Friedman (1989, A14) wrote an open letter to the national drug czar telling him:

Your mistake is failing to recognize that the very measures you favor are a major source of the evils you deplore. Of course the problem is demand, but it is not only demand, it is demand that must operate through repressed and illegal channels. Illegality creates obscene profits that finance the murderous tactics of the drug lords; illegality leads to the corruptions of law enforcement officials; illegality monopolizes the efforts of honest law forces so that they are starved for resources to fight the simpler crimes of robbery, theft and assault. Drugs are a tragedy for addicts. But criminalizing the use converts that tragedy into a disaster for society, for users and non-users alike.

Along the same lines, Richard Cowan in the *National Review* wrote that "the hysterical myths about marihuana . . . have led conservatives to condone massive programs of social engineering, interference in the affairs of individuals, monstrous bureaucratic waste" (cited in Bertram et al. 1996, 94). Bertram et al. (1996, 231–232) also cited a speech by George Schulz, secretary of state in the Reagan administration: "It seems to me we're not really going to get anywhere until we take the criminality out of the drug business and the incentives for criminality out of it. Frankly, the only way I can think of to accomplish this is to make it possible for addicts to buy drugs at some regulated place at a price that approximates their cost."

In the libertarian frame, drug war policies are expensive, socially harmful, and counterproductive in that they increase the level of violence in society as drug sellers compete for market turf. To protect constitutional liberties, libertarians are more concerned about drug prohibition than about drug abuse. Miron (2010) sums up the libertarian argument by noting, "Drug prohibition, at least when imposed at the federal level, is also hard to reconcile with constitutionally limited government." Taking drugs is a personal judgment, not something to be controlled by the government. People need factual information about the drugs to make that judgment. And if addiction is the consequence of their personal decision, then this, too, is the individual's responsibility.

A conspiratorial story line within the libertarian narrative suspects that the drug war continues because of entrenched interests of the drug war enforcement complex.

Drug War Enforcement Complex. In this story line, police departments, federal prosecutors, the Drug Enforcement Administration, prison guards, and others exploit the war on drugs for their own interests. The war on drugs allows law enforcement agencies to confiscate the assets of those convicted of drug use or drug trafficking. Boats, houses, cars, guns, real estate, money, and many other attractive assets are awarded to law enforcement agencies that only have to demonstrate "probable cause." Helicopter manufacturers, whose products are used in crop eradication efforts, might also be included as coconspirators in the drug war enforcement complex.

As Turnbull (2005, 134) diplomatically phrased it when writing about the Marihuana Tax Act of 1937, "No cotton farmer would admit that his opposition to the use of marijuana was based on his fear of competition from hemp, but any businessman who could not see a danger so obvious would not stay in business very long." It would also make conspiratorial sense if the pharmaceutical industry sought to preserve a market for its synthetic drugs, for the beer, wine, and liquor industries to preserve their markets for recreational inebriants, or for cigar and cigarette companies to ensure that tobacco products are the available smoke.

The conspiracy narrative sees DuPont Chemicals seeking to establish its own market for synthetic nylon in denying market share for hemp. A conspiracy story advanced by Herer (2000, 25-26) proposes that "in the mid-1930s, when the new mechanical hemp fiber stripping machines and machines to conserve hemp's high cellulose pulp finally became state-of-the-art, available and affordable, the enormous timber acreage and business of the Hearst Paper Manufacturing Division, Kimberly Clark (USA), St. Regis—and virtually all other timber, paper and large newspaper holding companies, stood to lose billions of dollars and perhaps to go bankrupt." Why? The new hemp-pulp technology for papermaking, invented in 1916 by Lyster Dewey and Jason Merrill of the U.S. Department of Agriculture (Herer 2000, citing *USDA Bulletin 404*), was now ready for production, thanks to the invention of the *decorticator,* a machine invented by George Schlichten that could strip the fiber from nearly any plant, leaving the pulp behind. According to a *Popular Mechanics* article, hemp was to become the new billion-dollar crop because of the invention of this labor-saving machine (article reproduced at http://www.druglibrary.org/schaffer/hemp/popmech1.htm).

Meanwhile, DuPont Chemicals had a patent on a new sulfate/sulfite process for making paper from wood pulp. The technology would allow Hearst Paper Manufacturing Division and other timber companies to produce very cheap paper. New developments in hemp technology threatened this advantage. Hence, entrenched interests destroyed the hemp industry in the United States, according to the conspiracy theory.

Indeed, the Marihuana Tax Act of 1937 was moved through Congress so swiftly that the editors of *Popular Mechanics* apparently did not realize such a bill was on the table until after the article had gone to press. "New Billion Dollar Crop" would be obsolete by the time it was published in February 1938. Indeed, William C. Woodward of the American Medical Association (AMA) said, "We cannot understand yet, Mr. Chairman, why this bill should have been prepared in secret for two years without any intimation, even to the profession, that it was being prepared" (quoted in Herer 2000, 194). The AMA had been told of the hearings two days in advance.

It is doubtful that many people were aware that the Ways and Means Committee was considering a law that would prohibit hemp. Deitch (2003) claims that the politicians who approved the Marihuana Tax Act did not understand that they were effectively outlawing hemp at the same time. In World War II, the navy was desperate for hemp, which was the predominant raw ingredient of lines used on vessels. (For a video of *Hemp for Victory* go to http://www.youtube.com /watch?v=Ne9UF-pFhJY.) "Most of them had been duped into believing they were taxing the use of an allegedly harmful drug—*'marijuana,'* to discourage its use" (Deitch 2003, 1). If Deitch is correct, it would have been a clever, albeit cynical, strategy to use a foreign-sounding name in the Marihuana Tax Act.

It seems the committee members were also ill prepared. Members of the committee had questions: Is this hashish? Is this sometimes called loco weed? Is this a harmful drug-producing weed? Are you describing a plant that has a rather large flower? Is it not Indian hemp? According to Anslinger, "We seem to have adopted the Mexican terminology, and we call it marihuana, which means good feeling" (Anslinger 1937).

The conspiracy narrative suspects behind-the-scenes manipulation of the rules of the game, which was played unfairly from the start. The central story line of the futility narrative is at the other end of the war on drugs' history; the war on drugs is simply not working.

D. Futility of Drug Policy

If rational antidrug policy is about what works, prognoses have long been gloomy. As Bertram et al. (1996, 15) claim, the typical drug organization can lose 70 to 80 percent of its product and remain profitable. Meanwhile, the drug industry in Bolivia employs 500,000 people, about 20 percent of the workforce (16). "Even in the face of mounting evidence from committee hearings, GAO reports, the media, and policy analysts that the drug war was failing, Congress acted not to challenge or change policy but to prod the president to do more and to spend more in the war on drugs" (134–135). Degenhardt et al. (2008, 1062) found that drug-use rates vary from country to country, but that, in general, the United States ranked among the highest levels of use of all drugs. As these researchers concluded:

> The use of drugs seems to be a feature of more affluent countries. The US, which has been driving much of the world's drug research and drug policy agenda, stands out with higher levels of use of alcohol, cocaine, and cannabis, despite punitive illegal drug policies, as well as . . . a higher minimum legal alcohol drinking age than many comparable developed countries. The Netherlands, with a less criminally punitive approach to cannabis use than the US, has experienced lower levels of use, particularly among younger adults. Clearly, by itself, a punitive policy towards possession and use accounts for limited variation in nation-level rates of illegal drug use.

Mayo (2008) wrote about a paramilitary raid on a home in Pembroke Pines, Florida, on June 12, 2008, that resulted in the shooting death of Vincent Hodgkiss: "Is this what America really wants from its War on Drugs? Thanks to this investigation, a 46-year-old father ended up dead and police recovered about an ounce-and-a-half of pot."

Shields (2006) writes that information technology is diminishing the ability of enforcement agencies to combat drug trafficking. Increased surveillance has led to countermeasures on the part of drug organizations and money launderers. Similarly, closing off one port of entry for drugs only means that drug organizations will shift their business to another port of entry. Illegal crops eradicated in one region will show up in another. Despite efforts by the United States to substitute alternate crops for coca, poppy, and marijuana in poor countries, where most of the illegal product is grown, and despite attempts to interdict shipments of product headed for or entering the United States and despite efforts to track down and arrest drug dealers, availability remains high, demand remains high in the United States, and the drug business continues to flourish in an underground market that yields high profits and much corruption (Bertram et al. 1996, 11–12). "Most analysts agree that scare tactics (the fear arousal approach) and moral appeals (preaching to students about the evils of drinking, smoking, and using drugs and exhorting them to abstain) do not work. Exaggerating the dangers of drugs undermines the credibility of the message and often backfires, encouraging experimentation" (175). The rational analyst would argue that programs of eradication, interdiction, improving drug treatment, outlawing a product useful as medical treatment and as an agricultural crop, and disrupting drug markets should show success or should yield the stage to something that does work. Continuing on an expensive path that does not lead to where we want to go would make no pragmatic sense. According to the Global Commission on Drug Policy (2011, 2): "The global war on drugs has failed, with devastating consequences for individuals and societies around the world. Fifty years after the initiation of the UN Single Convention on Narcotic Drugs, and 40 years after President Nixon launched the US government's war on drugs, fundamental reforms in national and global drug control policies are urgently needed. Vast expenditures on criminalization and repressive measures directed at producers, traffickers and consumers of illegal drugs have clearly failed to effectively curtail supply or consumption."

In the futility narrative, drug policy reform is needed.

IV. SUMMARY

In this appendix, I have identified various ways drug policy has been framed in the United States. Each of these framing narratives presents its own distinguishing facts, logic, and ideography, although the futility narrative frequently intermingles with other decriminalization narratives. The dominant coalitions of narratives that have been put into practice through public policy are not made up of rationality so much as salient imagery and values. Typologies have implications, to be sure, but the important lesson from this appendix is not that the narrative category schema is true. Rather, narratives are comprised of coherent constellations of emotions, values, stereotypes, cultural habits, and symbolic connotations that give public policy shape and texture. Emotions and values share discursive space with logic and facts to distinguish one narrative from another.

In rational policy analysis, the aim is to get the facts right and present a logically consistent and coherent argument. This is the story line that has difficulty gaining traction in the drug policy discourse. Discourse theory helps us to see why such aspirations can be unrealistic, why the facts are not as tightly bound to reality as one might prefer, and why coherence is not only a logical proposition but also an ideographic phenomenon. Information that is used in drug policy formulation includes facts and rational analyses and, also, powerful images, ideographs, and story lines, but the differences among the different narratives laid out above are not reducible to empirical differences or analytical differences.

Appendix 2 illustrates how the environmental policy discourse has unfolded quite differently from the drug policy discourse, and, yet, environmental policy and administration, too, are infused with ideographic narratives, underscoring the symbiosis between narrative and practice.

Appendix 2
Environmental Policy Discourse

The environmental policy discourse picked up steam in the 1960s with books about overpopulation, dead birds, and finite worldwide resources. Aside from civilization's ever-necessary attention to waste disposal and clean water, an earlier conservation movement that began in the second half of the 19th century was perhaps America's first policy-relevant articulation of environmental sensibilities. Literary appreciations of nature written by authors such as Henry David Thoreau, John Burroughs, and John Muir must surely have laid some of the ideographic groundwork for the policy changes that were to come later. This appendix will touch on three episodes of environmental discourse: the conservation movement epitomized by the establishment of the U.S. Forest Service, the environmental movement that culminated in the formation of the Environmental Protection Agency (EPA), and the 1980s' antigovernmental trend, whose emblematic policy debate may be the Sagebrush Rebellion during the Reagan administration, which moved the conversation from decentralization toward privatization and market solutions.

I. THE CONSERVATION NARRATIVE

One important precursor to the creation of the U.S. Forest Service in 1905 was the establishment of Yellowstone National Park in 1872 during the presidency of

Ulysses S. Grant. A political rationale justifying such a land set aside was articulated a year later. The concern of Franklin Hough, first in a paper, "On the Duty of Governments in the Preservation of Forests," presented at the 1873 meeting of the American Association for the Advancement of Science (AAAS) and subsequently in an AAAS committee report, led to the congressional creation of a special Department of Agriculture office, whose job was to assess the quality and conditions of forests in the United States.

The office so requested by AAAS was established in 1876; in 1881, the office expanded into the Division of Forestry. Its guiding narrative, as expressed by Hough, included themes of efficiency, profits, and benefits—and preservation of the existing woodlands. Hough seemingly affirmed both the conservation narrative and the preservationist narrative in his remarks to the Chamber of Commerce (*New York Times* 1884).

By the time of Grover Cleveland's second term in office (1893–1897), the president had been granted the power to set aside land (by a law passed in 1891), and Cleveland used this power to set aside 21 million acres of forest reserves in a decree issued within the last two weeks of his presidency (*New York Times* 1897). The next president, William McKinley, kept the land in the public domain by turning it over to the Interior Department; he assigned it to its General Land Office (Egan 2009, 34). The General Land Office had a reputation for favoring mining and timber barons. Few were prosecuted for the alleged corruption that took place. For example, according to the *New York Times* (1895), "The Commissioner decided that John Y. McBride was entitled, by reason of having filed mining claims thereto, to land in the City of Tacoma, Washington, valued at $2,000,000. . . . The idea of fraud in connection with the proceedings is spurned by the Washington officials." McKinley subsequently hired Gifford Pinchot to look into the western lands (Egan 2009, 34) and soon thereafter appointed him head of the U.S. Department of Agriculture's Division of Forestry, a tiny unit of government by today's standards, but one that would in seven years become the U.S. Forest Service. McKinley was assassinated in 1901, and the vice president, Theodore Roosevelt, became president. Roosevelt turned out to be a Progressive who both challenged the mining and timber barons and promoted conservation. His remarks to the joint session of Congress on December 6, 1904, presaged the now-familiar idea of sustainability as well as the establishment of the U.S. Forest Service: "It is the cardinal principle of the forest-reserve policy of this Administration that the reserves are for use. Whatever interferes with the use of their resources is to be avoided by every possible means. But these resources must be used in such a way as to make them permanent" (T. Roosevelt 1904).

Roosevelt was advocating a conservation ethic, a sustainability argument of sorts, as opposed to a preservation ethic, which would be less keen on exploiting forestlands for their timber and mineral resources. He expressed concern for the water supply and for the timber supply and sought authorization from Congress to set aside additional land reserves for the preservation of certain species. Various executive orders and offices had preceded the establishment of the U.S. Forest Service, but there had been little public administration of the forests because the staff was so small. No corps of forest rangers checked the commercial exploitation of public resources by private interests. Nonetheless, the U.S. Forest Service was established in the U.S. Department of Agriculture in 1905, after the conservation narrative had been advancing for some time.

As the United States industrialized its economy, the value of nature—material, aesthetic, and transcendent—gained in public perception, even as these same natural resources were increasingly despoiled by the machinations of industrial capitalism. The conservation ethic was heterodox, mostly a mix of Progressive anticorruption instincts along with an expanded preservation/conservation awareness. John Muir added an aesthetic tone to the preservationist vision: nature provides an opportunity for refreshment and to escape modernity as well as the apathy generated by luxury (Muir 1901). The property-rights argument that Pinchot would make seemed a logical extension of conservation and anticorruption values: "The earth, I repeat, belongs of right to all its people, and not to a minority, insignificant in numbers but tremendous in wealth and power" (quoted in Egan 2009, 66).

Rep. Joseph Cannon, member of the House of Representatives from Illinois, opposed Theodore Roosevelt's conservation efforts. "Not one cent for scenery!" he urged (quoted in Egan 2009, 68). Meanwhile, Sen. Weldon Heyburn maintained that forestry was not a science. "Forestry has been fostered as a policy to uphold the leisurely, lazy dignity of a monarch" (quoted in Egan 2009, 69). With that kind of resistance, sufficiently small appropriations for the Forest Service ensured that when fire broke out in the West and rangers needed resources, rangers had to pay for supplies from their own pockets (Egan 2009).

Under Roosevelt's successor, William H. Taft, Congress passed a law making it illegal for the U.S. Forest Service to publicize itself, possibly affecting the public policy discourse and undermining constituency development and support. Hence, even after the U.S. Forest Service operations commenced (which is to say the conservation narrative was institutionalized), its enemies in Congress persisted in their resistance to the narrative's further expansion.

But the very effective Gifford Pinchot, who wrote *The Fight for Conservation,* published in 1910, engaged the resistance. "We, the American people, have come into the possession of nearly four million square miles of the richest portion of the earth. It is ours to use and conserve for ourselves and our descendants, or to destroy. The fundamental question which confronts us is, What shall we do with it?" (Pinchot 1910, 5). His book reads like an agriculture-age precursor to the 1972 Club of Rome report *The Limits to Growth* (Meadows et al. 1972). Pinchot (1910, 9–10) expressed concerns about overgrazed land; that some iron ore fields have been exhausted; that oil is sometimes burned just to get rid of it; that inefficient coal-burning trains waste coal; and that soil erosion was getting worse: "No seeing man can travel through the United States without being struck with the enormous and unnecessary loss of fertility by easily preventable soil wash." Pinchot was prescient in his concern that "vast amounts of gas continue to be poured into the air and great quantities of oil into the streams" (7). There was also a telltale Progressivism in his advocacy: "In addition to the principles of development and preservation of our resources there is a third principle. It is this: The natural resources must be developed and preserved for the benefit of the many, and not merely for the profit of a few" (46). He also advocated that "conservation means the greatest good to the greatest number for the longest time" (48) and that "the special interests must be put out of politics" (147). "The alliance between business and politics is the most dangerous thing in our political life. It is the snake that we must kill" (133).

The conservation narrative received a lucky boost from a huge forest fire that took place in August 1910. This "great burn" was a spectacular fire (actually, several fires attributable to an exceedingly dry summer season that year combined with high winds) that damaged 100 square miles of forest in Washington, the Idaho panhandle, and Montana (*New York Times* 1910a). Newspapers lamented the loss of life, especially the lives of forest rangers, the loss of lumber, the destruction of mines, and the destruction of numerous western towns (*New York Times* 1910b). Pinchot made narrative use of the fire by criticizing the members of Congress who had been working to undermine the U.S. Forest Service. "The men in Congress like Heyburn, Carder, and Mondell, who have made light of the efforts of the Forest Service to prepare itself to prevent such a calamity as this, have, in effect, been fighting on the side of the fires as against the general welfare" (quoted in *New York Times* 1910c). Heyburn's counterargument was that the fires were God's will and that the rangers themselves were an impediment. "The presence of thousands of men in the forest whose principal industry is to establish the necessity for their employment will always constitute a menace to the forest" (quoted in Egan 2009, 242). The narratives, brought into play immediately before and after the establishment of the U.S. Forest Service, played out again, but with more force and more diversity, in the political contests of the 1960s surrounding the establishment of the U.S. EPA and the Council on Environmental Quality some 65 years later.

II. REGULATORY ENVIRONMENTALISM
INSTITUTIONALIZED

In environmental policy discourse, interesting and powerful ideographs have been deployed by a diverse array of spokespersons. In the 1960s, Stewart Brand tried to persuade the National Aeronautical and Space Administration (NASA) to release the photographic image of planet Earth, only rumored to exist, that was taken from a satellite. Indeed NASA eventually released it and soon the image was on the cover of Brand's *Whole Earth Catalog.* The lonely looking bluish Earth was set against an infinite, empty black background on the oversized catalog, giving a sense that Earth was a lonely planet, indeed. A couple years after that, the image appeared again on the Earth Day flag. Earth Day, a national environmental teach-in led by Sen. Gaylord Nelson of Wisconsin, took place on April 22, 1970. The National Environmental Policy Act was established at the beginning of the year and the U.S. EPA was established later that same year.

The legislative environmental agenda followed cultural shifts brought about by polemics such as Rachel Carson's 1962 *Silent Spring,* a book about pesticide poisoning of birds, nature in general, and humans in particular. This episode is described in chapter 5, as an illustration of the sort of policy discourse that fueled environmentalism's successful narrative. The book contained vivid ideographic imagery as well as careful research.

Scientific research also came into play in the public discourse through other high-impact books. Paul Ehrlich's *The Population Bomb* was published in 1968 and provided a Malthusian interpretation of population growth. In 1968 there were 3.5 billion people on the earth and double that by fall 2011. Overpopulation of the planet has long been a concern to pessimists willing to perform the demographic calculations. Famine, disease, war, and social stress are the images that are associated with overpopulation distress. While Ehrlich's dismal assessment was a "face the facts" sort of treatise, his predictions of mass starvation in the 1970s and 1980s were overreaching.

Population bomb or not, a national discourse increasingly attuned to environmental concerns became a political force that President Nixon did not ignore. The national mood continued to assert itself into public policy discourse. Esposito (1970) was uncompromising in his criticism of federal environmental policy immediately preceding the establishment of the EPA. Some pollutants—asbestos, beryllium, and cadmium—should not be tolerated at all, and "the only remedy is an outright prohibition of all emissions, even if this might mean closing down some business establishments" (19). Government agencies came under attack for underperformance. The inadequacy of the National Air Pollution Control Administration, particularly in its deference to state enforcement of air quality standards, was deemed inadequate, even perverse, by outspoken critics (for example, Landy, Roberts, and Thomas 1994). The Council on Environmental Quality was established by legislation passed in 1969, and on January 1, 1970, President Nixon signed the National Environmental Policy Act. Later that year, the EPA was established by a reorganization proposal from Richard Nixon that was endorsed by Congress.

William D. Ruckelshaus was the first administrator of the EPA. According to Ruckelshaus (1993, 1), "The big difference between the early 1960s (when we struggled to get anything done in Indiana) and the 1970s was the shift of public opinion. There was no public support for the environment in Indiana in the late 1950s and early 1960s. . . . If there wasn't some kind of odor problem or obvious health problem in a town, local people would not support action against a local industry, because that threatened jobs . . . [and] there was really no overall federal enforcement to speak of."

When the EPA was first organized, it was a collection of policy implementation units gathered together from among different governmental organizations. O'Leary (1993, 5) lists the various units, mainly from the Departments of Interior; Health, Education, and Welfare; and Agriculture, that comprised the agency. Before the EPA was established, Congress had already passed a number of legislative initiatives including the Water Quality Act of 1965, which gave the U.S. Department of Health, Education, and Welfare the power to establish water quality standards, and the 1966 Clean Water Restoration Act, which allocated money for construction of sewage systems. "We had 15 agencies or pieces of agencies all under our umbrella. We had separate and overlapping geographic regions for air, water, and solid waste, which we had to bring together in one regional structure" (Ruckelshaus 1993, 2). "We had to organize the agency headquarters in Washington. We inherited a pesticides agency from the Agriculture Department which was created to stop what the Department of Health, Education, and Welfare (HEW) was doing to regulate pesticides. All of a sudden, both were under one roof!" (2).

One can sympathize with the EPA's organizational challenge; a propesticide agency that had been housed in the U.S. Department of Agriculture had to be merged into the same organization as a pesticide regulatory office from the Department of Health, Education, and Welfare (Ruckelshaus 1993). In addition to organizational problems, there were unanswered scientific and technological questions. While some of the worst pollutants had been identified, "we certainly didn't know all of them, nor their effects at very high levels" (Ruckelshaus 1993, 4). And even if the most dangerous pollutants could be identified, there was little knowledge about how to control their effects or how costly it would be. Such operational uncertainties were overshadowed by Ruckelshaus's need to establish the credibility of the EPA, and to demonstrate "the willingness of the central government, and the political process, to respond to the legitimate demands of the people" (5). Ruckelshaus selected DDT as one way of doing this.

The already in-place institutional milieu, not only industrial corporations and their lobbying groups, offered resistance. Ruckelshaus (1993, 5–6) reported experiencing difficult relations with the White House and the Office of Management and Budget (OMB). Agreements that had been settled had to be renegotiated, including, for example, the standards for implementing the Clean Air Act. State regulatory agencies, too, resisted EPA efforts (8).

The EPA's relations with the environmental movement, as one might expect, were positive, as the agency accepted the environmental movement's agenda as its own mission. "But I would say that the agency's relationship, and my own relationship with environmental groups, was *much more* positive at the start of EPA than ten years later" (Ruckelshaus 1993, 9, emphasis in original). "The early days were a lot of fun. We really operated effectively and had a good group of people, with whom we worked closely. There were antagonisms and strife like you always have in institutions; but by and large everybody thought they were attached to a cause larger than themselves. We worked *very* hard, long hours, but had a lot of fun doing it" (Ruckelshaus 1993, 12, emphasis in original).

The EPA was constantly in court, sometimes being sued by the industry it was trying to regulate, sometimes by environmentalists trying to force the EPA to do a better job of enforcing its mandate, and sometimes itself suing a local government for failing to follow EPA mandates. O'Leary (1993, 9) regards the impact of courtroom litigation as problematic: "Clearly litigation is not the best way to formulate environmental policy or to determine our nation's environmental priorities." However, it may also be the case that litigation is merely discourse by other means in a different setting, yet another way of articulating a narrative to change practice. By 1993, the discourse had gathered in technical and managerial concerns and regulatory operations. If the thrill had diminished a bit over time, the competency of the agency had improved, according to Ruckelshaus (1993), who had been appointed EPA administrator for a second time in the 1980s during the Reagan administration. "I think the agency was *better* able to deal with problems confronting it when I returned than when I started, simply because the staff had accumulated an awful lot of *experience* dealing with the issues. The people in the agency also had a better appreciation of the *enormous* impact their decisions had on the society; an impact not only on the environment and on public health, but also on jobs and on the economy" (16, emphasis in original). The Progressive legacy of activist government implicitly promises to not waste taxpayer dollars in the process. This promise was more in evidence during Ruckelshaus's second term at the EPA, with more emphasis on effectiveness, efficiency, and less burdensome ways of achieving outcomes. Another legacy of activist government of the period of institutionalization is the notion of participation. Environmental agencies were explicit about citizen participation, and this was nowhere more in evidence than in the establishment of the National Environmental Protection Act.

The National Environmental Policy Act (NEPA) created the Council on Environmental Quality, a small office of the White House. According to Hill (1973), NEPA has been the basis for much environmental litigation because it enabled citizens to file lawsuits without having to show substantive personal injury; citizens could have standing by speaking in the public interest against environmentally dubious practices. Hill (1976) credited the environmental impact statements, required under NEPA, for providing the bases for much litigation. Importantly, a negative analysis in an environmental impact statement does not prevent a project from going forward. However, the studies of environmental impacts make the project a very public one that can raise concerns and controversies, invite explanation and intelligibility, and problematize phenomena previously unacknowledged in the discourse. The environmental impact statements led to expanded deliberation regarding the effects of projects once taken for granted, such as highway construction and chemical spraying. Dubious practices became subject to the white glare of public awareness. Sen. Henry M. Jackson, chair of the Interior Committee, inserted the requirement of environmental impact statements at the last minute before the Senate vote (Kenworthy 1972). However, it was not obvious in 1970 that NEPA would be enforced at all. According to Kenworthy (1970): "The Sierra Club, a leading conservation organization, accused the Nixon Administration today of either ignoring or circumventing the Environmental Policy Act when it recommended passage of a bill to increase logging in the national forests. And Senator Edmund S. Muskie, chairman of the Senate Subcommittee on Air and Water Pollution, also expressed concern as to whether there had been 'compliance' with the new law."

Yet, NEPA survived, as did the sometimes-tenuous Council on Environmental Quality. The enactment of NEPA was followed by the establishment of the EPA in 1970, as already noted, and also by the Water Pollution Control Act Amendments of 1972, the banning of DDT by the EPA in 1972, the Environmental Pesticide Control Act of 1972, the Noise Pollution and Abatement Act of 1972, and the Coastal Zone Management Act of 1972. A succession of other environmental measures followed the flurry of the early 1970s. O'Leary (1993, 13–14) lists the numerous statutes that the EPA implemented. According to Hill (1975), NEPA introduced revolutionary changes to the semisecret way bureaucracies had operated in the past, as well as changes created by enabling citizen lawsuits and the proliferation of environmentally sensitive legislation among states and cities throughout the United States.

However, in 1973, the U.S. Congress expressed its impatience with environmental impact statements and the years of litigation they generated; it declared by majority vote that NEPA requirements had been met and that Alaskan pipeline construction should begin (Hill 1975). As Hill (1974) reported in the *New York Times,* "After four years of intense controversy, the Department of the Interior issued a permit today for the building of a 789-mile pipeline to take oil from Alaska's North Coast to the ice-free port of Valdez." (It seems appropriate to note here that the oil spill 14 years later, in 1989, from the ruptured *Exxon Valdez* oil tanker on its way out of Valdez's Prince William Sound, served as tragic affirmation of the potential for environmental disaster.) The passage of the oil pipeline legislation was an early signal that the environmental narrative was meeting strong resistance; policy implementation itself had generated political controversy. A turning point was in the making. An antigovernment mood was beginning to change the public policy discourse.

III. AN ANTIGOVERNMENT MOOD

Environmental advocates interpreted Reagan-era environmental policy with apprehension. Little (2004) quoted select representatives of the environmental movement as they reflected back on the 1980s.

- "The Reagan administration adopted an extraordinarily aggressive policy of issuing leases for oil, gas, and coal development on tens of millions of acres of national lands—more than any other administration in history, including the current one" (David Alberswerth, Wilderness Society).
- "Never has America seen two more intensely controversial and blatantly antienvironmental political appointees than Watt and Gorsuch" (Greg Wetstone, Natural Resources Defense Council).

A conflict was in process. Because environmental concerns among the public were aroused in the 1980s, "environmental organizations experienced an enormous corresponding growth spurt" (Ingram, Colnic, and Mann 1995, 123). The Reagan administration was intent on providing regulatory relief to its business constituency; its OMB put procedures in place reducing regulatory effort. According to Sibbison (1985), reporting on these OMB procedures, "Before he was elected president, Ronald Reagan complained that the Environmental Protection Agency lacked an understanding of industry's problems. In his five years in the Oval Office, he has changed all that. Today industry executives help rewrite some EPA regulations before they go into effect, giving corporations more influence over the nation's environmental policies than ever before." This was part of what Ripley and Franklin (1991, 48) referred to as "a concerted effort to put and keep the bureaucracy under its thumb and to discourage the normal semi-autonomous relations between bureaus, interest groups, and congressional subcommittees." The fierce political contest, which also saw reduced budgets and reduced staff in regulatory agencies, was fueled by differing ideological assumptions about the proper role of government. As to which narrative came to dominate, regulatory or antigovernment, Ripley and Franklin (104) surmised: "In short, the political warfare over protective regulation produced a stalemate. Programmatically, each side scored some victories." Strong regulation and privatization were both prominent; some commentators tried to merge the two narratives by advocating management reform.

A. Administration Can't Shake Politics

Focusing less on the highly contested politics of environmental regulation, Rosenbaum (1995, 221–222) instead questioned the administrative style and environmental values of regulatory agencies such as the EPA and the Office of Surface Mining and Enforcement (OSME). Rosenbaum (223) surmised that environmental innovation in the federal bureaucracy had "gone awry." The regulatory bureaucracy had been overly politicized and therefore needed structural and legal insulation from politics. So-called command and control regulatory mechanisms should be displaced by market strategies (for example, cap and trade). Rosenbaum further laments "partisan, ideologically inspired, and conceptually circumscribed literature," (233) while hoping for conceptual sophistication in the environmental policy and administration literature. The end value for Rosenbaum (233) is "the protection and preservation of environmental vitality." However, this wish presupposes a consensus on environmental values—a consensus that exists only within the environmental discourse coalition. The environmental narrative continues to run up against the antigovernmental narrative. "Getting government off our backs" was part of the environmental discourse, as a clear and vivid expression of antiregulatory sentiment. Rosenbaum's focus on performance and goals could not patch over the political conflict inherent in the competition between the two narratives. As a political move, shifting the discourse to performance and goals was an attempt at expressing environmental aspirations in operational rather than overtly political terms—as a "how" question rather than a "what" question. The familiar call for Congress to write unambiguous laws also shifts the conversation to operations, even when writing precise statutes is not politically feasible. O'Leary (1993) suggests further that Congress reform itself.

The academic predilection for more rationality contrasts with the nonrational political environment in which environmental agencies originate. The so-called Sagebrush Rebellion of the 1980s exemplified the continued political contest over environmental regulation.

B. Sagebrush Rebellion

This movement was a reaction against the environmental influence on federal land policy in the 1970s, and it took place in the context of a narrative revision of what conservation means (Cawley 1993). Preservationists had gained influence, and land-use practices were changing. Sagebrush Rebels, to the contrary, were advocates of commodity production on public lands. "The Sagebrush Rebellion appears to have been an authentic political movement deriving support from a diverse group of people who believed that federal land management policies had become overly responsive to environmental preservation values" (Cawley 1993, 14). Preservationists rejected the instrumentalism of conservationists, who advocated wise use and planned development. Without either narrative winning that particular debate within the environmental movement, together they had been winning the larger debate. Grazing lands now competed with outdoor recreation; wilderness designations restricted the commercial use of public lands. In opposition, the Sagebrush Rebellion tapped into an antigovernment regulation narrative, a states' rights narrative, and an economic development narrative with respect to public lands.

This tension between preservationist values and the Sagebrush Rebellion created an opening for an even more robust antigovernmental narrative, the privatization movement. Though outright sale of public lands did not come about, the terms of the debate shifted not toward states' rights but toward a broader antigovernment market fundamentalism.

Narrative dominance is a relative term; dominance is situational and time specific. Though market fundamentalism was on the ascent, environmental regulation was firmly established through its institutionalization in the form of the EPA. Nonetheless, the specifics of practices and methods (for example, cap-and-trade proposals) were up for discussion.

IV. ENVIRONMENTALISM AS CONTESTABLE NARRATIVE

Both preservation and conservation are long-enduring environmental narratives, the former usually attributed to John Muir and the latter to Gifford Pinchot. So far these two narratives have been presented as minor divergences in the larger environmental narrative. This difference became acute in the years preceding the construction of the O'Shaughnessy Dam (aka the Hetch Hetchy Dam) in Hetch Hetchy Valley outside of San Francisco. Muir opposed it, while Pinchot favored it. The eventual decision to build the dam signaled the dominance of the conservation narrative in environmental discourse. Preservationism's aesthetic, transcendentalist approach would leave nature undisturbed, but the conservation narrative fit the times: science, instrumentalism, and engineering were heralding the rise of modernity. The early mission of the U.S. Forest Service was inspired by Pinchot's conservation approach, which more readily accommodated the decision some eight years later to proceed with the water project in the Hetch Hetchy Valley. An invading narrative came crashing in on environmentalisms of all types during the presidency of Ronald Reagan. This free market narrative was sometimes described as privatization. Its catchy slogan, as delivered by Reagan on the campaign trail, was "get government off our backs." Both the Sagebrush Rebellion and environmentalism were confronted with a high-velocity and rapidly changing counternarrative. While the failed attempt to sell off government assets was called privatization, privatization strategies— many successfully implemented—were part of a much larger parallel narrative about market fundamentalism, a narrative with powerful antiregulation story lines and antigovernment ideography.

References

Adams, Frank S. 1933. "Swing to Prohibition Repeal Came Suddenly after Long Fight." *New York Times.* Feb. 21. Online archives.

Anonymous. 2002. "The Importance of Prevention: Plea from a Young Laudanum Addict." In David F. Musto, ed., *Drugs in America: A Documentary History.* New York: New York University Press, pp. 226–228.

Anslinger, H. J. 1937. "Statement of H. J. Anslinger." http://www.druglibrary.org/schaffer/hemp/taxact/anslng1.htm, accessed June 28, 2009.

Anslinger, H. J., with Courtney Ryley Cooper. 2002. "The Danger of Marijuana: Assassin of Youth." In David F. Musto, ed., *Drugs in America: A Documentary History.* New York: New York University Press, pp. 433–440.

Bailey, Mary Timney. 1992. "Do Physicists Use Case Studies? Thoughts on Public Administration Research." *Public Administration Review* 52 (1): 47–54.

Barley, Stephen R., and Pamela S. Tolbert. 1997. "Institutionalization and Structuration: Studying the Links between Action and Institution." *Organization Studies* 18 (1): 93–118.

Barthes, Roland. 1972. *Mythologies.* Translated by Annette Lavers. New York: Hill and Wang.

———. 1975. *S/Z.* Translated by Richard Miller. New York: Hill and Wang.

———. 1977a. *Elements of Semiology.* Translated by Annette Lavers and Colin Smith. New York: Hill and Wang.

———. 1977b. "Rhetoric of the Image." In Stephen Heath, ed. and trans., *Image Music Text*. London: Fontana Press, pp. 32–51.

Baumgartner, Frank, and Bryan Jones. 1993. *Agendas and Instability in American Politics*. Chicago: University of Chicago Press.

Beecher, Lyman. 2002. "Six Sermons on the Nature, Occasions, Signs, Evils and Remedy of Intemperence." In David F. Musto, ed., *Drugs in America: A Documentary History*. New York: New York University Press, pp. 44–86.

Belville, Russ. 2008. "Record Number of Americans Arrested for Marijuana." http://blog.norml.org/2008/09/15/872721-marijuana-arrests-in-2007-up-52-from-2006/, citing FBI report "Crime in the United States 2007," accessed Sept. 6, 2011.

Bertram, Eva, Morris Blachman, Kenneth Sharpe, and Peter Andreas. 1996. *Drug War Politics: The Price of Denial*. Berkeley: University of California Press.

Biographical Directory of the United States Congress 1774-Present. http://bioguide.congress.gov/scripts/biodisplay.pl?index=m000818, accessed Aug. 19, 2010.

Bonnie, Richard J., and Charles H. Whitebread. 1974. *Marihuana Conviction: A History of Marihuana Prohibition in the United States*. Charlottesville: University Press of Virginia.

Bourdieu, Pierre. 1977. *Outline of a Theory of Practice*. Cambridge: Cambridge University Press.

Brecher, Edward M. 1972. *Licit and Illicit Drugs; The Consumers Union Report on Narcotics, Stimulants, Depressants, Inhalants, Hallucinogens, and Marijuana—Including Caffeine*. Boston: Little Brown.

Brody, Jane E. 1969. "Attacks on Use of DDT Increasing." *New York Times*. Apr. 30. Online archives.

Carson, Rachel. 1962. *Silent Spring*. New York: Houghton Mifflin.

Cawley, R. McGreggor. 1993. *Federal Land, Western Anger: The Sagebrush Rebellion & Environmental Politics*. Lawrence: University Press of Kansas.

Chandler, Daniel. 2002. *Semiotics: The Basics*. London: Routledge.

Cobb, Roger W., and Charles D. Elder. 1973. "The Political Uses of Symbolism." *American Politics Quarterly* 1 (3): 306–338.

———. 1976. "Symbolic Identifications and Political Behavior." *American Politics Research* 4 (3): 305–332.

"Coincidence?" 1975. *Traverse City (MI) Record-Eagle*. Aug. 4, p. 4.

Common Sense for Drug Policy. 2009. "How Experts Rate Problem Substances." http://www.drugwarfacts.org, accessed Aug. 10.

Cornwath, Tom, and Ian Smith. 2002. *Heroin Century*. London: Routledge.

"Crack Kids: Their Mothers Used Drugs, and Now It's the Children Who Suffer." 1991. *Time Magazine*, May 13, 19.

Davidson, Donald. 2001. *Inquiries into Truth and Interpretation,* 2nd ed. New York: Oxford University Press.

Dawkins, Richard. 1989. *The Selfish Gene,* 2nd ed. New York: Oxford University Press.

Degenhardt, Louisa, Wai-Tat Chiu, Nancy Sampson, Ronald C. Kessler, James C. Anthony, Matthias Angermeyer, Ronny Bruffaerts et al. 2008. "Toward a Global View of Alcohol, Tobacco, Cannabis, and Cocaine Use: Findings from the WHO World Mental Health Surveys." *PLoS Med* 5 (7): 1054–1067.

Deitch, Robert. 2003. *Hemp—American History Revisited: The Plant with a Divided History.* New York: Algora Publishing.

Department of Health and Human Services. 2008. *National Survey on Drug Use and Health.* http://www.icpsr.umich.edu/icpsrweb/SAMHDA/studies/23782/detail.

Dewey, John. 1997. *The Influence of Darwin on Philosophy and Other Essays.* Amherst, NY: Prometheus Books.

Diamond, Jared M. 2005. *Collapse: How Societies Choose to Fail or Succeed.* New York: Viking.

Drugwarfacts.org. 2010. "Crime—Tables: Total, Marijuana and Drug Arrests by Year." *http://www.drugwarfacts.org/cms/Marijuana#Total,* accessed Dec. 1, 2011.

Duncan, David F. 2002. "Drug Use by Workers, Does it Reduce Productivity?" Paper presented at the annual meeting of the American Public Health Association, Nov. 11, Philadelphia, PA.

Edelman, Murray. 1977. *Political Language: Words that Succeed and Policies that Fail.* New York: Academic Press.

———. 1988. *Constructing the Political Spectacle.* Chicago: University of Chicago Press.

Egan, Timothy. 2009. *The Big Burn: Teddy Roosevelt & the Fire That Saved America.* New York: Houghton Mifflin.

Esposito, John. 1970. *Vanishing Air: The Ralph Nader Study Group Report on Air Pollution.* New York: Grossman Publishers.

Falco, Mathea. 1992. *The Making of a Drug-Free America.* New York: Times Books.

FBI Uniform Crime Report. 2010. "Crime in the United States 2009." United States Department of Justice, Washington, DC, Sept., Table 29.

Fischer, Frank. 2003. *Reframing Public Policy: Discursive Politics and Deliberative Practices.* New York: Oxford University Press.

———. 2009. *Democracy & Expertise: Reorienting Policy Inquiry.* New York: Oxford University Press.

Foucault, Michel. 1970. *The Order of Things.* New York: Pantheon Books.

———. 1979. "On Governmentality." *Ideology and Consciousness* 6 (Autumn): 8–21.

———. 1982. *The Archaeology of Knowledge & the Discourse on Language.* Translated by A. M. Sheridan Smith. New York: Pantheon Books.

———. 1994. "The Subject and Power." In James D. Faubion, ed., *Power,* vol. 3,

The Essential Works of Foucault, 1954–1984, trans. Robert Hurley and others. New York: New Press.

———. 1995. *Discipline and Punish*. Translated by Alan Sheridan 1977. New York: Vintage Books.

Fox, Charles J., and Hugh T. Miller. 1995. *Postmodern Public Administration: Toward Discourse*. Thousand Oaks, CA: Sage.

———. 1997. "Positivism." In Jay Shafritz, ed., *International Encyclopedia of Public Policy and Administration*. Boulder, CO: Westview, pp. 1718–1723.

Friedman, Milton. 1989. "An Open Letter to Bill Bennett." *Wall Street Journal*. Sept. 7, pp. A1, A14.

Friedrich, Carl Joachim. 1940. "Public Policy and the Nature of Administrative Responsibility." In C. Friedrich and E. S Mason, eds., *Public Policy*. Cambridge, MA: Harvard University Press, pp. 3–24.

Gadamer, Hans-Georg. 1996. *Truth and Method*, 2nd rev. ed. New York: Continuum.

Giddens, Anthony. 1984. *The Constitution of Society: Outline of the Theory of Structuration*. Berkeley: University of California Press.

Global Commission on Drug Policy. 2011. ~~War~~ *On Drugs: Report of the Global Commission on Drug Policy*. June. http://www.globalcommissionondrugs.org.

Glynos, Jason. 2008. "Ideological Fantasy at Work." *Journal of Political Ideologies* 13 (3): 275–296.

Glynos, Jason, and David Howarth. 2007. *Logics of Critical Explanation in Social and Political Theory*. London: Routledge.

Goodsell, Charles T. 2011. *Mission Mystique: Belief Systems in Public Agencies*. Washington, DC: CQ Press.

Gottweis, Herbert. 2007. "Rhetoric in Policy Making: Between Logos, Ethos, and Pathos." In Frank Fischer, Gerald J. Miller, and Mara S. Sidney, eds., *Handbook of Public Policy Analysis: Theory, Politics, and Methods*. Boca Raton, FL: CRC Press.

Gueras, Dean, and Charles Garofalo. 2005. *Practical Ethics in Public Administration*, 2nd ed. Vienna, VA: Management Concepts.

Gusfield, Joseph R. 1981. *The Culture of Public Problems*. Chicago: University of Chicago Press.

Hajer, Maarten A. 1993. "Discourse Coalitions and the Institutionalization of Practice: The Case of Acid Rain in Great Britain." In Frank Fischer and John Forester, eds., *The Argumentative Turn in Policy Analysis and Planning*. Durham, NC: Duke University Press, pp. 43–76.

———. 2005. "Coalitions, Practices and Meaning in Environmental Politics: From Acid Rain to BSE." In David Howarth and Jacob Torfing, eds., *Discourse Theory in European Politics: Identity, Policy and Governance*. Hampshire, UK: Palgrave Macmillan, pp. 297–315.

Hastings, Annette. 1998. "Connecting Linguistic Structures and Social Practices:

A Discursive Approach to Social Policy Analysis." *Journal of Social Policy* 27 (2): 191–211.

Hatfield, Elaine, John T. Cacioppo, and Richard L. Rapson. 1994. *Emotional Contagion.* Cambridge: Cambridge University Press.

Hawkes, Terence. 1977. *Structuralism and Semiotics.* Berkeley: University of California Press.

Heclo, Hugh. 2008. *On Thinking Institutionally.* Boulder, CO: Paradigm.

Helmer, John. 1975. *Drugs and Minority Oppression.* New York: Seabury Press, p. 31.

Herer, Jack. 2000. *The Emperor Wears No Clothes: The Authoritative Historical Record of Cannabis and the Conspiracy Against Marijuana,* 11th ed. Oakland, CA: Quick American Archives. Also available at http://www.jackherer.com.

Higdon, Hal. 1969. "Obituary for DDT (in Michigan)." *New York Times.* July 6. Online archives.

Hill, Gladwin. 1973. "Environmental Movement Registers Gains in 3 Years." *New York Times.* Apr. 9. Online archives.

———. 1974. "Interior Department Issues Permit for the Building of Alaskan Oil Pipeline." *New York Times.* Jan. 24. Online archives.

———. 1975. "Midpoint of 'Environmental Decade': Impact of National Policy Act Assessed." *New York Times.* Feb. 18. Online archives.

———. 1976. "'70 Environmental Policy Act Is Found Generally Successful." *New York Times.* July 3. Online archives.

Hilts, Philip J. 1994. "Is Nicotine Addictive? It Depends on Whose Criteria You Use." *New York Times.* Aug. 2. Online archives.

Himmelstein, Jerome L. 1983. *The Strange Career of Marihuana: Politics and Ideology of Drug Control in America.* Westport, CT: Greenwood Press.

Hoffer, Eric. 2006. *The Passionate State of Mind: And Other Aphorisms.* Titusville, NJ: Hopewell Publications.

Huffington, Arianna. 2009. "Ending the War on Drugs: The Moment is Now." *Huffington Post.* May 14. http://www.huffingtonpost.com.

Human Rights Watch. 2009. "Decades of Disparity: Drug Arrests and Race in the United States." New York: Human Rights Watch.

Hummel, Ralph P. 1991. "Stories Managers Tell: Why They Are as Valid as Science." *Public Administration Review* 51 (1): 31–41.

Imas, J. M. 2005. "Rational Darkness: Voicing the Unheard in the Modern Management Discourse of Chile." *Administrative Theory & Praxis* 27 (1): 111–133.

Ingram, Helen M., David H. Colnic, and Dean E. Mann. 1995. "Interest Groups and Environmental Policy." In James P. Lester, ed., *Environmental Politics & Policy: Theories and Evidence,* 2nd ed. Durham, NC: Duke University Press, pp. 115–145.

Ingram, Helen, and Anne L. Schneider. 1995. "Social Construction (Continued): Response." *American Political Science Review* 89 (2): 441–446.

Ingram, Helen, Anne L. Schneider, and Peter deLeon. 2007. "Social Construction and Policy Design." In Paul A. Sabatier, ed., *Theories of the Policy Process*, 2nd ed. Cambridge, MA: Westview, pp. 93–126.

James, Jennifer. 1998. "Crack Kids: Cocaine's Living Legacy." *Do It Now Foundation.* Catalog no. 177, July.

John, Peter. 2003. "Is There Life after Policy Streams, Advocacy Coalitions, and Punctuations: Using Evolutionary Theory to Explain Policy Change?" *Policy Studies Journal* 31 (4): 481–498.

Jones, Bryan D., and Frank R. Baumgartner. 2005. *The Politics of Attention.* Chicago: University of Chicago Press.

Jones, Michael D., and Mark K. McBeth. 2010. "A Narrative Policy Framework: Clear Enough to Be Wrong." *Policy Studies Journal* 38 (2): 329–353.

Kaufman, Herbert. 1960. *The Forest Ranger: A Study in Administrative Behavior.* Baltimore, MD: Johns Hopkins University Press.

Kaufman, Leslie. 2011. "U.S. Proposes New Forest Management Plan." *New York Times.* Feb. 11, p. A19.

Kennedy, David M. 1980. *Over Here: The First World War and American Society.* New York: Oxford University Press.

Kenworthy, E. W. 1970. "Sierra Club and Muskie Accuse Administration of Disregarding New Environmental Policy Act." *New York Times.* Feb. 22. Online archives.

———. 1972. "A Showdown on Environmental Policy." *New York Times.* July 4. Online archives.

Kettl, Donald F. 2001. *The Transformation of Governance: Public Administration for Twenty-First Century America.* Baltimore, MD: Johns Hopkins University Press.

Kinder, Douglas Clark. 1992. "Shutting Out the Evil: Nativism and Narcotics Control in the United States." In William O. Walker, ed., *Drug Control Policy: Essays in Historical and Comparative Perspective.* University Park: Pennsylvania State University Press, pp. 117–137.

Kingdon, John W. 1984. *Agendas, Alternatives, and Public Policies.* New York: HarperCollins.

Krebs, Albin. 1975. "Harry J. Anslinger Dies at 83; Hard-Hitting Foe of Narcotics." *New York Times.* Nov. 18. Online archives.

Kuhn, Thomas. 1970. *The Structure of Scientific Revolutions*, 2nd ed. Chicago: University of Chicago Press.

Kurtz, Ernest. 1979. *Not-God: A History of Alcoholics Anonymous.* Center City, MN: Hazeldon.

Kyvig, David E. 2000. *Repealing National Prohibition*, 2nd ed. Kent, OH: Kent State University Press.

Laclau, Ernesto. 2005. *On Populist Reason.* London: Verso Press.

Lakoff, George. 2004. *Don't Think of an Elephant: Know Your Values and Frame the Debate—The Essential Guide for Progressives.* White River Junction, VT: Chelsea Green Publishing Company.

Lakoff, George, and Mark Johnson. 2003. *Metaphors We Live By,* 2nd ed. Chicago: University of Chicago Press.

Landy, Marc K., Marc J. Roberts, and Stephen R. Thomas. 1994. *The Environmental Protection Agency: Asking the Wrong Questions from Nixon to Clinton.* New York: Oxford University Press.

Lasswell, Harold D. 1970. "The Emerging Conception of the Policy Sciences." *Policy Sciences* 1 (1): 3–14.

Latour, Bruno. 2005. *Reassembling the Social: An Introduction to Actor-Network-Theory.* New York: Oxford University Press.

Lieberman, Robert C. 1995. "Social Construction (Continued) Reply." *American Political Science Review* 89 (2): 437–441.

Lindesmith, Alfred R. 1965. *The Addict and the Law.* Bloomington: Indiana University Press.

Little, Amanda. 2004. "A Look Back at Reagan's Environmental Record." *Grist.* June 10. http://www.grist.org/article/griscom-reagan/.

Lynch, Lorrie. 1975. "Tennis Teacher Fired, Questions Why." *Traverse City (MI) Record-Eagle.* Aug. 2, p. 1.

Lyons, Derek E., Andrew G. Young, and Frank C. Kell. 2007. "The Hidden Structure of Overimitation." *Proceedings of the National Academy of Sciences* 104 (50): 19751–19756.

Lyons, Richard D. 1967. "DDT Levels Held Wildlife Threat: Study in Long Island Finds Tissue Residues Lethal." *New York Times.* May 12. Online archives.

Majone, Giandomenico. 1992. *Evidence, Argument, and Persuasion in the Policy Process.* New Haven: Yale University Press.

Markham, James M. 1972. "President Calls For 'Total War' on U.S. Addiction." *New York Times.* Mar. 21. Online archives.

Mayo, Michael. 2008. "Pembroke Pines Shooting Raid: Trash Yields Probable Cause." *Sun-Sentinel.* June 26. http://weblogs.sun-sentinel.com/news/columnists/mayo/blog/2008/06/pembroke_pines_shooting_raid_t.html#more.

McGee, Michael C. 1980. "The 'Ideograph': A Link between Rhetoric and Ideology." *Quarterly Journal of Speech* 66 (1): 1–16.

McWilliams, John C. 1990. *The Protectors: Harry J. Anslinger and the Federal Bureau of Narcotics, 1930–1962.* Newark: University of Delaware Press.

Mead, George H. 1967. *Mind, Self, and Society: From the Standpoint of a Social Behaviorist.* Chicago: University of Chicago Press.

Meadows, Donella H., Dennis L. Meadows, Jorgen Randers, and William W. Behrens III. 1972. *The Limits to Growth.* New York: Universe Books.

Meier, Kenneth. 1994. *The Politics of Sin: Drugs, Alcohol, and Public Policy.* Armonk, NY: M. E. Sharpe.

Miller, Hugh T. 1975. "Marijuana and the Law." *Traverse City (MI) Record-Eagle.* July 31.

———. 1994. "Post-Progressive Public Administration: Lessons from Policy Networks." *Public Administration Review* 54 (4): 378–386.

Miron, Jeffrey A. 2010. "The Tea Party and the Drug War." *National Review Online.* June 7. http://www.nationalreview.com/articles/229902/tea-party-and-drug-war/jeffrey-miron.

Muir, John. 1901. *Our National Parks.* Boston: Houghton Mifflin. See also http://www.yosemite.ca.us/john_muir_writings/our_national_parks/.

Musto, David F. 1999. *The American Disease: Origins of Narcotics Control.* New York: Oxford University Press.

———, ed. 2002. *Drugs in America: A Documentary History.* New York: New York University Press.

Nadelmann, Ethan. 2010. "Obama Takes a Crack at Drug Reform." *Nation.* Sept. 13.

Nagel, Thomas. 1989. *The View from Nowhere.* New York: Oxford University Press.

National Drug Control Strategy. 2009. White House (Bush administration) Report to the Congress, January. http://www.whitehousedrugpolicy.gov/publications/policy/ndcs09/2009ndcs.pdf, accessed June 6, 2009.

National Institute on Drug Abuse and National Institute on Alcohol Abuse and Alcoholism. 1992. *The Economic Costs of Alcohol and Drug Abuse in the United States 1992.* Rockville, MD: U.S. Department of Health and Human Services, Sept. 1998, pp. 1–10.

New York Times. 1884. "Managing the Forests." Jan. 15. Online archives.

———. 1895. "Believe That the Decision Will Stand: Officers of the Land Office Think Tacoma Must Lose Her Land." Feb. 23. Online archives.

———. 1897. "New Forest Reservations: Proclamations by the President Covering 21,379,840 Acres." Feb. 23. Online archives.

———. 1910a. "100 Mile Tract is in Grip of Fires." Aug. 22. Online archives.

———. 1910b. "Over 50 Dead; Fire Rages On." Aug. 23. Online archives.

———. 1910c. "Pinchot Places Blame for Fires." Aug. 27. Online archives.

———. 1926a. "Kills Six in a Hospital: Mexican, Crazed by Marijuana, Runs Amuck with Butcher Knife." Feb. 21. Online archives.

———. 1926b. "Marijuana Smoking Is Reported Safe: Hemp Leaves, Classed in Some States with Drugs, Tested by Canal Zone Committee." Nov. 21. Online archives.

———. 1932. "Say Drys' 'New Era' Disproved Hopes: Women Wets Contrast Forecasts of Cut in Crime and Other Benefits with Facts Today." Jan. 16. Online archives.

———. 1969. "Ban on DDT Sales Voted in Michigan." Apr. 16. Online archives.

———. 1994. "Blowing Smoke at Congress." Apr. 17. Online archives.

Nutt, David, Leslie A. King, William Saulsbury, and Colin Blakemore. 2007. "Development of a Rational Scale to Assess the Harm of Drugs of Potential Misuse." *The Lancet* 369 (9566): 1047–1053.

O'Leary, Rosemary. 1993. *Environmental Change: Federal Courts and the EPA.* Philadelphia: Temple University Press.

Oplinger, Jon. 1990. *The Politics of Demonology: The European Witchcraze and the Mass Production of Deviance.* Cranbury, NJ: Associated University Presses.

Ospina, Sonia M., and Jennifer Dodge. 2005. "It's about Time: Catching Method up to Meaning: The Usefulness of Narrative Inquiry in Public Administration Research." *Public Administration Review* 65 (2): 143–157.

Ostrowski, James. 1990. "Thinking about Drug Legalization." In David Boaz, ed., *Crisis in Drug Prohibition.* Washington, DC: Cato Institute, pp. 45–76.

Perry, Mark J. 2007. "Crack vs. Powder Cocaine in Pictures." http://mjperry.blogspot .com/2007/10/crack-vs-powder-cocaine-in-pictures.html, accessed Nov. 22, 2008.

Pfeffer, Jeffrey. 1992. *Managing with Power: Politics and Influence in Organizations.* Boston: Harvard Business School Press.

Pinchot, Gifford. 1910. *The Fight for Conservation.* New York: Doubleday.

Polanyi, Karl. 1944/2001. *The Great Transformation: The Political and Economic Origins of Our Time.* Boston: Beacon Press.

Poovey, Mary. 1998. *A History of the Modern Fact: Problems of Knowledge in the Sciences of Wealth and Society.* Chicago: University of Chicago Press.

Popular Mechanics. 1938. "New Billion-Dollar Crop." http://www.druglibrary.org /schaffer/hemp/popmech1.htm, accessed Nov. 29, 2011.

Pressman, Jeffrey, and Aaron Wildavsky. 1973. *Implementation: How Great Expectations are Dashed in Washington: Or, Why It's Amazing That Federal Programs Work at All, This Being a Saga of the Economic Development Administration as Told to Two Sympathetic Observers Who Seek to Build Morals on a Foundation of Ruined Hopes.* Berkeley: University of California Press.

Radin, Beryl. 2006. *Challenging the Performance Movement: Accountability, Complexity, and Democratic Values.* Washington, DC: Georgetown University Press.

Rein, Martin, and Donald Schön. 1993. "Reframing Policy Discourse." In Frank Fischer and John Forester, eds., *The Argumentative Turn in Policy Analysis and Planning.* Durham, NC: Duke University Press, pp. 145–166.

Reynolds, Grace. 2009. "Drug Treatment Program Compliance and Resistance Activities during Implementation of California's Proposition 36." *Journal of Health and Human Services Administration* 32 (1): 51–73.

Richards, Stephen C., and Michael T. Avery. 2000. "Controlling State Crime in the United States of America: What Can We Do about the Thug State?" In Jeffrey

Ian Ross, ed., *Varieties of State Crime and Its Control.* Monsey, NY: Criminal Justice Press, pp. 31–58.

Ripley, Randall B., and Grace A. Franklin. 1991. *Congress, the Bureaucracy, and Public Policy,* 5th ed. Pacific Grove, CA: Brooks Cole.

Robinson, Matthew B., and Renee G. Scherlen. 2007. *Lies, Damned Lies, and Drug War Statistics: A Critical Analysis of Claims Made by the Office of National Drug Control Policy.* Albany: State University of New York Press.

Rochefort, David A., and Roger W. Cobb. 1993. "Problem Definition, Agenda Access, and Policy Choice." *Policy Studies Journal* 21 (1): 56–71.

Roe, Emery. 1994. *Narrative Policy Analysis: Theory and Practice.* Durham, NC: Duke University Press.

Roosevelt, Franklin D. 2002. "Campaign Address on Prohibition." In David F. Musto, ed., *Drugs in America: A Documentary History.* New York: New York University Press, pp. 151–153.

Roosevelt, Theodore. 1904. "To the Senate and House of Representatives." *Infoplease.* http://www.infoplease.com/t/hist/state-of-the-union/116.html#axzz0xGat2S61, accessed Aug. 19, 2010.

Rosenbaum, Walter A. 1995. "The Bureaucracy and Environmental Policy." In James P. Lester, ed., *Environmental Politics & Policy: Theories and Evidence,* 2nd ed. Durham, NC: Duke University Press, pp. 206–241.

Rosenbloom, David H. 2000. *Building a Legislative Centered Public Administration.* Tuscaloosa: The University of Alabama Press.

Ruckelshaus, William D. 1993. "Ruckelshaus Interview." Washington, DC: U.S. Environmental Protection Agency, Office of Administration, Management, and Organization Division.

Sabatier, Paul A. 1988. "An Advocacy Coalition Framework of Policy Change and the Role of Policy-Oriented Learning Therein." *Policy Sciences* 21 (2/3): 129–168.

Sabatier, Paul A., and Hank C. Jenkins-Smith. 1993. *Policy Change and Learning: An Advocacy Coalition Approach.* Boulder, CO: Westview.

Sapir, Edward. 1929. "The Status of Linguistics as a Science." *Language* 5 (4): 207–214.

Saussure, Ferdinand de. 1983. *Course in General Linguistics.* Peru, IL: Open Court Publishing.

Schafer, Raymond P., and other members of the National Commission on Marihuana and Drug Abuse. 1972. *The Report of the National Commission on Marihuana and Drug Abuse—Marihuana: A Signal of Misunderstanding.* http://www.druglibrary.org/schaffer/library/studies/nc/ncmenu.htm, accessed Aug. 17, 2010.

Schaler, Jeffrey A. 2002. *Addiction Is a Choice.* Peru, IL: Open Court Publishing.

Schattschneider, E. E. 1960. *The Semi-Sovereign People: A Realist's View of Democracy in America.* New York: Holt, Rinehart and Winston.

Schneider, Anne, and Helen Ingram. 1993. "The Social Construction of Target Populations." *American Political Science Review* 87 (2): 334–346.

———, eds. 2005. *Deserving and Entitled: Social Constructions and Public Policy.* Albany: State University of New York Press.

Schön, Donald A., and Martin Rein. 1994. *Frame Reflection: Toward the Resolution of Intractable Policy Controversies.* New York: Basic Books.

Selznick, Philip. 1996. "Institutionalism 'Old' and 'New.'" *Administrative Science Quarterly* 41 (2): 270–277.

Shepard, Edward M., and Thomas J. Clifton. 1998. "Drug Testing and Labor Productivity: Estimates Applying a Production Function Model." Le Moyne College Institute of Industrial Relations, Research Paper No. 18. Syracuse, NY: Le Moyne University.

Shields, Peter. 2006. "When the 'Information Revolution' and the U.S. Security State Collide: Money Laundering and the Proliferation of Surveillance." *New Media & Society* 7:483–512.

Sibbison, Jim. 1985. "Whose Agency Is It, Anyway? How OMB Runs EPA." *Washington Monthly,* pp. 19+. *Academic OneFile,* accessed July 30, 2010.

Simon, Herbert A. 1976. *Administrative Behavior: A Study of Decision Processes in Administrative Organization.* New York: Free Press.

Somers, Margaret R. 1994. "The Narrative Constitution of Identity: A Relational and Network Approach." *Theory and Society* 23 (5): 605–649.

———. 2008. *Genealogies of Citizenship: Markets, Statelessness, and the Right to Have Rights.* Cambridge: Cambridge University Press.

Sommerness, Marty. 1975. "Residents Agree: Ford Visit Exciting." *Traverse City (MI) Record-Eagle.* July 15, p. 3.

Spicer, Michael W. 2010. *In Defense of Politics in Public Administration: A Value Pluralist Perspective.* Tuscaloosa: The University of Alabama Press.

Stivers, Camilla. 1993. *Gender Images in Public Administration: Legitimacy and the Administrative State.* Newbury Park, CA: Sage.

Stone, Deborah. 1997. *Policy Paradox: The Art of Political Decision Making.* New York: W. W. Norton and Company.

Tarde, Gabriel. 1903. *The Laws of Imitation.* Translated by Elsie Clews Parsons. New York: Henry Holt and Company.

Tesh, Sylvia Noble. 1988. *Hidden Arguments: Political Ideology and Disease Prevention Policy.* New Brunswick, NJ: Rutgers University Press.

———. 2000. *Uncertain Hazards: Environmental Activists and Scientific Proof.* Ithaca, NY: Cornell University Press.

Thomas, Chuck. 1996. "Marijuana Arrests and Incarceration in the United States." *Marijuana Policy Report* 1 (9): 7. Washington DC: Marijuana Policy Project.

Tipple, Terence J., and J. Douglas Wellman. 1991. "Herbert Kaufman's Forest Ranger Thirty Years Later: From Simplicity to Homogeneity to Complexity and Diversity." *Public Administration Review* 51 (5): 421–428.

Tonry, Michael. 1990. "Research on Drugs and Crime." In Michael Tonry and James Q. Wilson, eds., *Drugs and Crime*. Chicago: University of Chicago Press.

Torgerson, Douglas. 2003. "Democracy through Policy Discourse." In Maarten A. Hajer and Hendrik Wagenaar, eds., *Deliberative Policy Analysis: Understanding Governance in the Network Society*. Cambridge: Cambridge University Press.

Traditional Values.org. 2009. "Barney Frank Wants America to Be Woodstock Nation." *Right Side News*. July 4. http://www.rightsidenews.com/200907045336/culture -wars/barney-frank-wants-america-to-be-woodstock-nation.html, accessed July 5, 2009.

Turnbull, Andy. 2005. *The System: It's How the World Works*. Toronto: Red Ear Publishing.

Tzfadia, Erez, Yagil Levy, and Amiram Oren. 2010. "Symbolic Meanings and the Feasibility of Policy Images: Relocating Military Bases to the Periphery in Israel." *Policy Studies Journal* 38 (4): 723–744.

Urbina, Ian. 2009. "House Approves Bill That Would Ease Federal Grip on Washington." *New York Times*. Dec. 10, p. A25.

U.S. Sentencing Commission. 2007. *Report to the Congress: Cocaine and Federal Sentencing Policy*. http://www.ussc.gov/r_congress/cocaine2007.pdf.

Wagenaar, Hendrik. 2011. *Meaning in Action: Interpretation and Dialogue in Policy Analysis*. Armonk, NY: M. E. Sharpe.

Waldo, Dwight. 1948/2007. *The Administrative State: A Study of the Political Theory of American Public Administration*. New Brunswick, NJ: Transaction Publishers.

Weber, Max. 1978. *Economy and Society*. Edited by Guenther Roth and Claus Wittich. Berkeley: University of California Press.

Weick, Karl. 1979. *Social Psychology of Organizing*, 2nd ed. New York: McGraw-Hill.

Weiss, Carol H. 1977. "Research for Policy's Sake: The Enlightenment Function of Social Science Research." *Policy Analysis* 3 (4): 531–545.

Whorf, Benjamin Lee. 1997. "The Relation of Habitual Thought and Behavior to Language." In John B. Carroll, ed., *Language, Thought, and Reality: Selected Writings of Benjamin Lee Whorf*. Cambridge, MA: Technology Press of Massachusetts Institute of Technology, pp. 134–159.

Wildavsky, Aaron. 1987. *Speaking Truth to Power: The Art and Craft of Policy Analysis*. New Brunswick, NJ: Transaction Publishers.

Wilkinson, Tracy. 2009. "Mexico Moves Quietly to Decriminalize Minor Drug Use." *Los Angeles Times*. June 21. http://www.latimes.com/features/health/medicine/la -fg-mexico-decriminalize21–2009jun21,0,6336338.story.

Williams, Edward H. 1914. "Negro Cocaine 'Fiends' are a New Southern Menace:

Murder and Insanity Increasing among Lower Class Blacks Because They Have Taken to 'Sniffing' Since Deprived of Whisky by Prohibition." *New York Times Sunday Magazine.* Feb. 8. Online archives, SM12.

Wittgenstein, Ludwig. 2009. *Philosophical Investigations.* Translated by G. E. M. Anscombe, P. M. S. Hacker, and Joachim Schulte. Rev. 4th ed., translated by P. M. S. Hacker and Joachim Schulte. London: Blackwell.

Wood, Horatio C. 1869. "On the Medical Activity of the Hemp Plant, as Grown in North America." *Proceedings of the American Philosophical Society* 11 (81): 226–232.

Woodwell, George M., Charles F. Wurster Jr., and Peter A. Isaacson. 1967. "DDT Residues in an East Coast Estuary: A Case of Biological Concentration of a Persistent Insecticide." *Science* 156 3776 (May 12): 821–824.

Woolley, John T., and Gerhard Peters. *The American Presidency Project.* Hosted by University of California Santa Barbara. http://www.presidency.ucsb.edu/ws/index .php?pid=7908, accessed Aug. 5, 2009.

Wright, Hamilton. 2002. "The Shanghai Commission's Recommendations on Cocaine." In David F. Musto, ed., *Drugs in America: A Documentary History.* New York: New York University Press, 368–379.

Index